Always Ready:
A Christian Mandate

Gordon S. Jackson

M☩ Zion Ridge Press
Books Off the Beaten Path

www.MtZionRidgePress.com

Mt Zion Ridge Press LLC
295 Gum Springs Rd, NW
Georgetown, TN 37366

https://www.mtzionridgepress.com

ISBN 13: 978-1-962862-89-9
Published in the United States of America
Publication Date: December 15, 2025
Copyright: © 2025 Gordon S. Jackson

Editor-In-Chief: Michelle Levigne
Executive Editor: Tamera Lynn Kraft
Cover art design by Tamera Lynn Kraft
Cover Art Copyright by Mt Zion Ridge Press LLC © 2025

Semper paratus
Always prepared

In omnia paratus
Prepared for anything

Dedication

For Hazel and Sophie

Table of Contents

PART 1

1: Introduction

Whether we know it or not, we humans are always getting ready, trying to prepare for whatever may be coming next. We're getting ready for school, for work, for the Thanksgiving trip to Grandma's house. We prepare for all the tasks and responsibilities of being a grown-up, whether the weekly routine of taking out the trash or the seasonal tasks like installing your car's snow tires. Then there's that moment that in one form or another comes to all of us: preparing for our end, when a doctor may tell us, "I'm sorry but it's time to put your affairs in order. There's nothing more we can do for you."

For Christians, though, this perpetual need for getting ready takes on a different dimension. We frame "getting ready" or "preparing" in the light of God's presence and direction in our lives. And that makes a world of difference. So, the Christian college student seeking God's will pursues a major that she thinks will best equip her to serve God's Kingdom upon graduation. The Christian businessman will bring his faith to bear on every aspect of his dealings, with customers, employees, suppliers, and even the tax authorities. The Christian medical practitioner sees each patient not just as another statistic, but as one of God's own children, deserving of the respect and dignity that God Himself accords that person.

This book, then, is about how Christians, in all walks of life and at all stages of their Christian journey, are to live distinctively because of a simple reality: God expects us, at every moment, to be ready to "live Christianly," whether it is in the routine moments or the unexpected ones. God requires of us a mindset of being always prepared to live as His people, and to be prepared for anything.

Nothing makes this clearer than Jesus' own words, in the parable of the bridesmaids and the lamps, (Mt. 25:1-13), a curious story that we'll explore presently. In addition, Jesus tells us that we cannot know the hour of His return and therefore always need to be ready: "So you also must be ready, because the Son of Man will come at an hour when you do not expect Him." (Mt. 24:44)

But what does being "ready" or "prepared" entail for Christians? Embedded in this question are numerous related ones, such as:

- What precisely do we mean by "readiness"?
- How do we attain such "readiness"?
- What exactly are we to be ready for?

1

- Is readiness an all-or-nothing condition, as the parable of the bridesmaids suggests, or can we be partly or "sort of" ready?
- Are there lessons to be learned from Jesus' life and His own preparation for His ministry?
- And two ultimate questions, which are inextricably linked: How do I get ready for Jesus' second coming or, if I should die before His return, how do I prepare for my life's end?

No matter where you are in your Christian journey, this book offers reflections on these questions, among others, to help you better assess what kind and level of readiness God expects of you in your walk with Him.

~~~~~

All Scripture references are from the *New International Version* of the Bible, except where noted otherwise. Then there is the issue of inclusive language. Some quotes use "man," "mankind" and so on when referring to people in general. These quotes reflect earlier usage which characterizes contemporary English less and less. In keeping with this volume's commitment to present all sources as accurately as possible, I have included these entries with their original wording.[1]

My goal is to provide an array of fresh insights into our faith via the twin concepts of readiness and preparedness. How to use this book? You can dip into it wherever you want, reading the entries in whatever sequence you like. You may want to use these for your personal devotions. If you do, consider writing a brief response to each entry, especially in conjunction with other elements of your devotional time, such as prayer or Bible reading.

These entries may occasionally interpret Scripture differently from your own understanding. If that occurs, feel free to rely on your understanding of these Bible passages. But please don't let any such differences distract you from an entry's main point.

It's my hope that the insights that follow will enrich your own faith and help you to share the marvelous riches of God's Kingdom with those whose lives you will touch.

---

[1] The use of masculine pronouns to refer to God is done with due deference to concerns about inclusive language. Their use is not to assert that God is masculine. Where possible, attempts have been made to avoid masculine pronouns. But they have been included rather than resort to the heavy-handed artificiality of writing things like, "We seek to know who God is, how God deals with us, and what God wants to characterize our life together as God's people." Elsewhere, quoted material using these pronouns is left unchanged, respecting the need to accurately present these sources.

2: The Ten Bridesmaids

As a young boy in South Africa, I was a cub scout for a few years. One of the requirements at our weekly meetings was to have what was called a tickey, a small three-penny coin smaller than the US dime. The reason? That was the coin needed in the 1950s to make a call from a public telephone. As part of the scouting emphasis on always needing to "be prepared," we needed that tickey because you never knew when you might have to phone home. As I recall, I never had to use that tickey. But there was a certain satisfaction knowing I had one on hand if I needed it.

For much different reasons, we Christians ought also to be prepared, an idea Jesus drove home powerfully in His parable of the ten virgins or bridesmaids. As recounted in Matthew 25, Jesus' story highlights the contrasting states of readiness of two groups of women awaiting the groom's arrival. Their role was to accompany the groom with their lights—long poles with oil-soaked rags set alight, to illumine the way for the groom and his entourage. The oil in these lamps, according to the *New International Version* study notes, needed replenishing about every fifteen minutes.

As this short story unfolds, the hour gets later and all ten women fall asleep. But then comes the word that jars them into wakefulness. The bridegroom has arrived: "Come out to meet him!" Then we get to the crux of the parable. Five of the bridesmaids shake off their sleepiness, and ready themselves to accompany the bridegroom to the wedding banquet. The other five, however, don't have enough oil. Unprepared, they ask the others to share what they have, only to be rebuffed and told to go to their local oil sellers to top up their supplies. By the time they get to the banquet hall, the door's already shut and despite their pleas to be allowed in, the parable concludes with the sobering statement by the bridegroom: "Truly, I tell you, I don't know you.'"

The early church saw this parable as an admonition to Jesus' followers always to be ready for His return. That lesson is equally applicable to Christians today. While contemporary Christians, at least in the West, typically don't live in the expectation of Jesus' imminent return, if this parable were not enough incentive to do so, there are numerous passages elsewhere in the New Testament testifying that Jesus will return. In Matthew's gospel alone, for example, Jesus refers to His return nearly a dozen times.[2]

Besides being ready for Jesus' return, and not slacking off in our discipleship, what else can Christians today learn from this parable? We can identify six lessons.

First, there's the obvious point that these ten bridesmaids had no doubt that the groom would come. That wasn't at issue, even for the unprepared ones. The great unknown, however, was *when*. Some churches may go to what we think are extremes in obsessing over Jesus' return, even to the point of working out complex timetables and predictions of exactly when the second coming will occur. Flawed though these obsessive approaches may be, it's also likely that many of us err in the opposite direction and downplay Jesus' return, perhaps seeing it as some distant possibility rather than a firm promise. We may well need more of the bridesmaids' conviction and certainty that their groom would indeed show up.

Second, it's noteworthy that as the evening got later and later, the bridesmaids all fell asleep. But notice that Jesus doesn't suggest that they are at fault for doing so. He doesn't expect of us supra-human discipleship; we get tired, hungry, thirsty. He too got so exhausted that He could sleep through a storm on the Sea of Galilee. Instead, the issue is that when woken, half of them rubbed the sleep out of their eyes, perhaps took a quick bathroom break, and readied their lamps so they could play their crucial role in the wedding. The *New Jerome Bible Commentary* notes that "[A]bsolute vigilance is not so much the point as readiness."[3]

The unwillingness of the prepared bridesmaids to share with the others is our third point. At first glance, this seems selfish and even harsh. However, commentators tend to agree that this aspect of the story isn't about sharing or selfishness. Rather, it's emphasizing the need for us to have an individual relationship with God. As William Barclay puts it, "A man cannot borrow a relationship with God; he must possess it for himself."[4] The five wise bridesmaids were aware of their obligations to the groom, something they could not afford to undercut by sharing their oil. We don't know why the five unprepared bridesmaids had not planned ahead. But that is not the point of the parable, which is instead to emphasize the need for preparedness — something that the five negligent young women had failed in.

The fourth lesson relates to the element of surprise and the late hour of the groom's arrival. The groom comes at midnight, the darkest hour and least expected time. Who is up and about at that hour? Surely only

---

[2] See for example Mt. 16:27, 28; 24:27, 30, 37, 39, 44; 25:31; 26:64.
[3] *The New Jerome Commentary*, 668.
[4] William Barclay: *Daily Study Bible: Matthew vol. 2*, 320.

those set on robbery or other wrongdoing. Yet it is at this totally unpredictable time that the groom shows up.

In Matthew chapters 24 and 25 Jesus speaks about our need to anticipate and be ready for His second coming. For some of us, though, we may not have experienced His "first coming" in our lives, a lack that can be addressed by opening ourselves to His call and claim on our lives. Whether it is for this first encounter with Jesus, or for subsequent ones with Him as we walk beside Him in faith, we do well to remember that Jesus is the one who may come at the midnight of our lives, when we least expect His arrival.

That brings us to our fifth point. Being responsive to Jesus and the call of the Holy Spirit in our lives may not be easy. Even the wise bridesmaids would probably have preferred to go on sleeping, rather than heading out at midnight to serve the bridegroom. Craig Barnes warns us that opening ourselves to the Holy Spirit's leading comes with a risk: "The sudden arrival of the Holy Spirit into our lives is never what we had in mind. What we had in mind was a source of hope that was a little less painful and permitted us a whole lot more control. We didn't plan on loss, embarrassment or failure. We didn't plan on not reaching our dreams."[5] Well, not always. But readiness may lead us, with some reluctance, to places or involve tasks in God's service that we had never anticipated. The "how" and "when" of God's call may, as it was for the wise bridesmaids, not be our preferred way of doing things. The foolish ones, sadly, paid a severe price for letting the groom down at the critical moment. Their actions disappointed the groom to the point that they were excluded from the banquet.

The sixth and final lesson is perhaps the most intriguing. It concerns the focus of the ten bridesmaids: the arrival of the groom and the banquet that would follow, are both "good things," eagerly anticipated. Often when we focus on preparedness or planning, we emphasize the bad things that can happen. For example, it's prudent (and usually required by law) to have car and homeowner's insurance, to protect us if bad things happen. And if we're forward-thinking, we prepare for possible power outages, or other emergencies that can arise without warning. These are all negative scenarios that call for common sense actions in advance to cover "maybe" situations and lessen the toll they may take on us.

However, the contrast with the ten bridesmaids' situation is dramatic. Far from preparing to mitigate possible damage, they had the opportunity to prepare for something positive and eagerly awaited: their participation in the wedding proceedings. Those events were highly positive occasions in that culture—and ours as well, of course.

---

[5] Craig Barnes: *Yearning*, 114.

Their preparations were in anticipation of joy, as are ours when we get ready for positive events, like weddings, graduation ceremonies, or milestone birthdays. It's easy and obvious that these kinds of upcoming good things call for thinking ahead and preparedness. It's much harder to be ready for good things that are unexpected. Yet that is precisely the optimistic, positive outlook on every area of life that should characterize each Christian. No, we're not talking about a Pollyannaish, naïve or even self-deluding view of life that foolishly disregards life's hardships. Instead, the orientation of each Christian should be around a joyful recognition that God is in control of everything and that *in the long run* everything will work out well. As Paul puts it, "[W]e know that in all things God works for the good of those who love him, who have been called according to his purpose." (Rom. 8:28). Likewise, we have the assurance that God is interested in every detail of our lives, as Jesus assures us in Matthew 10:30: "And even the very hairs of your head are numbered." With that assurance of God's care for us, both in the short term and long term, we ought to be living lives expectant of good.

~~~~~

Notwithstanding these six lessons, Jesus adds a footnote to the parable that drives home the main point, in case we've missed it: "Therefore keep watch because you do not know the day or the hour." (Mt. 25:13) It is noteworthy that this parable is reinforcing Jesus' warnings about preparedness for His return that were outlined in the previous chapter in Matthew. Here He foreshadows in virtually identical wording the need for readiness when He says: "Therefore keep watch, because you do not know on what day your Lord will come." (Mt. 24:42)

How, though, does God expect us to emulate the behavior of the five wise bridesmaids? There are at least two ways, of equal importance. First, Jesus has a general expectation that His disciples will behave Christianly at all times, oriented to honoring Him and not bringing embarrassment or shame to His cause and His Kingdom. Then there's also the more general attitude we see in the wise bridesmaids: a readiness and openness to action, at any moment. Not only did they act when called upon to do so, they were ready. So too with us. At least in theory, we need to be oriented toward Jesus' call, at a moment's notice, to act in His service. It could be as simple as helping out a neighbor who has a sudden baby-sitting crisis, or as life-changing as answering God's call into pastoral or mission work. Like the wise bridesmaids, we have no doubt that responding to God's call will be both the obedient and fulfilling thing to do.

Which brings us to the crucial question, on which we will focus for the rest of this book: "What kind of readiness does God expect of us to do justice to His invitation to attend His heavenly banquet?"

3: So, What *Is* Christian Readiness?

"Are you ready, dear? We're going to be late for church."
"Our lawyer says we should be ready to go to trial in March."
"I need to get the kids ready for bed."
"I don't think she's ready for marriage; she's only eighteen."

Defining what we mean by "ready" seems self-evident. Likewise with its close synonym, "prepared." Each of these terms implies that action will follow or, to be more accurate, that some kind of action *may* follow. We assume that the couple will go to church, that we will go to trial in March, and that I will get the kids ready for bed. It's not clear, though, if the eighteen-year-old will in fact get married in the near future. Maybe, maybe not. But her state of readiness remains a question.

Getting ready suggests a wide range of preparatory activities, from getting dressed and heading out of the house to church, to the meticulous preparation our lawyer is undertaking. Ask anyone what they mean by "getting ready" and you're likely to get similar answers. It's not a mysterious or complicated concept. But what if we add the dimension of *Christian* readiness? What does "readiness" or "being prepared" imply for the Christian?

The parable of the ten bridesmaids makes clear that Jesus expects His followers to be ready at all times. Yes, we are to be ready for His second coming, for "the Son of Man will come at an hour when you do not expect Him." (Mt. 24:44) In addition, Christians have an expanded view of readiness that goes beyond the need to be on time for church or preparing for a trial or getting the children ready for bed. For we are at all times to be attuned to what God may require of us. That can come as a long-term calling, such as preparing for a career as a high school teacher or a pediatric nurse, for example. Alternatively, our openness to God's direction may play out as a Spirit-led impulse to stop in on old Mrs. Murphy to see how she's doing today.

In brief, Christian readiness requires us to be open to the whole gamut of possible Spirit-inspired actions that we could conceivably engage in. As Paul told the Colossians, "[W]hatever you do, whether in word or deed, do it all in the name of the Lord Jesus, giving thanks to God the Father through Him." (Col. 3:17)

So, whether it is as routine as getting the trash ready for tomorrow's pickup or dealing with an unexpected crisis like responding to your aging father who's had a stroke, we Christians are expected to infuse into *all* our actions and conduct a godliness that our non-Christian neighbor cannot easily understand.

In much of life it may appear we are just like that neighbor. We each have homeowner's and car insurance to be prepared for the unexpected and unwanted. Then, to prepare for the inevitable, Christians and non-Christians alike take out life insurance because they don't want to leave a surviving spouse with three children in a financial hole if they died prematurely.

Like a soldier who is on guard duty, we may spend much time being ready, in a general sense, for something that never happens. On the other hand, we need to be proactive and take every opportunity to proclaim and live out our faith in whatever way is appropriate. As Paul says, we are to "Preach the word; be *prepared* in season and out of season; correct, rebuke and encourage..." (2 Tim. 4:2, emphasis added)

How then shall we define "Christian readiness"? We can see it as always being primed to respond Christianly to any situation, prepared to act in a God-honoring way. Christian readiness therefore differs from a "generic" or "ordinary" readiness in at least three ways.

- Christians ought always to have a "God focus" in their predisposition to act or speak in a godly way. Advancing God's Kingdom is to be our driving force in all we say and do. It is as if we are permanently wearing God-tinted lenses and see everything in that light.

- A related concept is that Christian readiness transcends our self-interest. God's will, as best we can discern it, and not our personal preferences, should be our north star. Jesus' words in Matthew 6:33 come to mind here: "But seek first His kingdom and His righteousness, and all these things will be given to you as well."

- Finally, Christian readiness is shaped by a conviction that God is in charge. God is either directing the circumstances we face or, if we are encountering something bad, we know this has happened only because God permitted it. We can take comfort from the words of an unknown writer who said, "The will of God will never lead you where the grace of God cannot keep you."

~~~~~

The question arises, "What then should Christians be ready *for*? The general answer is found in the inscription at the beginning of this book: *Semper paratus/In omnia paratus*—"Always prepared/Prepared for anything." The more pointed, paraphrased answer for Christians is, "Always prepared for godly service/prepared for anything that God requires of us or permits to come our way." Oswald Chambers says, "Readiness for God means that we are ready to do the tiniest little thing or the great big thing, it makes no difference."[6]

So how do we attain such a state of readiness? Let us take a first step in answering that question by asking another: "How did Jesus prepare for His ministry?" That is the subject of our next chapter.

---

[6] Oswald Chambers: *My Utmost for His Highest*, April 18.

4: Preparation: Jesus' Example

We know little about Jesus' boyhood. But the gospels give us important clues about His preparation for ministry once He became an adult. Moreover, we can discern much from His ministry, which lasted about three years, regarding the way He readied Himself for that role. We can identify six ways in which He prepared. Together, these qualities form an unparalleled example for us to follow.

- His close walk with and dependence on His heavenly Father
- His vigorous prayer life
- His knowledge of Scripture
- His uncompromising resistance to temptation
- His teaching and mentoring ministry, preparing His disciples to spread the gospel after He left them, and
- His openness to Spirit-guided spontaneity.

Despite our frailties and fallenness, we are — at least in theory — able to emulate Jesus in each of these ways, which now merit brief attention.

Jesus' Close Walk With His Father: Admittedly, not even the most saintly among us can claim, as Jesus could, that "I and the Father are one." (Jn. 10:30) Even though Jesus was God incarnate, He had in common with us all the limitations of ordinary human beings like you and me. In choosing to "empty Himself" of His heavenly status, as Paul describes in the letter to the Philippians, Jesus "made Himself nothing." (Phil. 2:7) He knew hunger, fatigue, emotional anguish, and physical pain. Having freely chosen to take on a human body He also freely chose to depend on His heavenly Father in all aspects of His life, and especially for knowing God's will and direction. Jesus' will was thus truly in sync with that of God the Father. As He said, "Very truly I tell you, the Son can do nothing by Himself; He can do only what He sees His Father doing, because whatever the Father does the Son also does." (Jn. 5:19)

Jesus' Active Prayer Life: Jesus was constantly "in touch" with His Father, as we read repeatedly in the gospels. He knew He could not be adequately prepared for both His overall ministry as well as the day-by-day demands He faced without a heavy reliance on communion with His Father. In addition to His agonizing season of intense prayer in Gethsemane, we see over and over how Jesus took time to slip away from His disciples and the crowds for private prayer. For example, we read in

Matthew's gospel that "After He had dismissed them, He went up on a mountainside by Himself to pray." (Mt. 14:23) In Mark we learn that "Very early in the morning, while it was still dark, Jesus got up, left the house and went off to a solitary place, where He prayed." (Mk 1:35)

If we want to get a sense of what Jesus' prayer life must have been like, it's likely to have been exactly the opposite of what Robert McAfee Brown said: "Prayer for many is like a foreign land. When we go there, we go as tourists. Like most tourists, we feel uncomfortable and out of place. Like most tourists, we therefore move on before too long and go somewhere else."[7] Jesus, by contrast, would have felt this was His natural milieu, talking to His Father. He certainly wasn't a "tourist" in the land of prayer; nor would He have wanted to move on as soon as He could. Instead, His alone and intimate time with His Father was, among other things, a time of equipping for the day and days ahead.

Jesus' Mastery of Scripture: Perhaps the best-known example of Jesus' use of Scripture comes in His wilderness encounter with Satan, right after John baptizes Him. Having heard God's voice of approval, surely a spiritual high point at the outset of Jesus' ministry, He relies repeatedly on Scripture to ward off Satan's onslaught. With each of the three temptations, Jesus' knowledge of the Old Testament Scriptures equips Him to resist Satan's offers. We don't know at what stage in His life He began to acquire His knowledge of Scripture. Probably it began as a child, as we see evidence of His learning and knowledge when as a twelve-year-old He astonished the teachers in the temple: "Everyone who heard Him was amazed at His understanding and His answers." (Lk. 2:47)

Although it's not stated explicitly, we can reasonably infer that Jesus' "understanding and answers" were grounded in a thorough grasp of Scripture – preparation that proved indispensable in His subsequent ministry. A few examples of His reference to Scripture are when He talks to the Pharisees about marriage and divorce, citing Genesis (Mk. 10:2-12); in the Sermon on the Mount, quoting Exodus 20 (Mt. 5:21, 27); and Psalm 31:5 when He is on the cross (Lk. 23:46). He quotes from the Psalms more than from anywhere else, as well as from the books of Deuteronomy, Isaiah, Hosea and Malachi. He clearly knew the Scriptures thoroughly, knowledge that proved an essential building block in preparing for His ministry.

Jesus Resisted Temptation: We are so familiar with the story of Jesus' temptation in the wilderness that we may think that was the only occasion He had to resist evil. But as *The Interpreter's Bible* reminds us, "Temptation did not end for Jesus in the wilderness. It often recurred. It

---

[7] Quoted in Gordon S. Jackson: *Quotes for the Journey, Wisdom for the Way*, 122.

came again with terrific power when the cross neared, in Gethsemane. But He had made answer in the wilderness, and chosen His path: 'Not my will, but thine, be done.'"[8]

Given the intense pressure Jesus faced in Gethsemane, knowing the horrific reality that lay ahead, we might be inclined to say that the wilderness experience was just "practice temptation," in other words a training exercise to prepare Him for what lay ahead with the crucifixion. But that would do an injustice to the ordeal of His one-on-one showdowns with Satan, from each of which He emerged victorious.

Then there were whatever other temptations He must surely have faced, of which Scripture has no record. Yet beginning with the ordeal in the wilderness (and perhaps earlier, in His youth) Jesus repeatedly resisted temptation so that He was prepared to take on the Devil himself, again and again. The result, said the writer to the Hebrews, is that "…we do not have a high priest who is unable to empathize with our weaknesses, but we have one who has been tempted in every way, just as we are—yet He did not sin." (Heb. 4:15)

Jesus' Preparation of Others: Nearly forty references in the gospels mention Jesus teaching His disciples and the crowds. There's no doubt that each gospel author is at pains to stress the teaching aspect of Jesus' ministry. He was not a pontificating Messiah; He was a *teaching* Messiah. He wasn't some guru sharing pious platitudes; He was God incarnate introducing the good news of God's Kingdom to the world. His followers, including the disciples, struggled at times to grasp His teaching, but there's no doubt that He instilled in them enough of His message for the Holy Spirit to work with, so that this small group of people helped to turn the world upside down with their proclamation of the gospel.

Spirit-Guided Spontaneity: We read repeatedly in the gospels about people interrupting Jesus with their dire needs. Think of blind Bartimaeus, for example. Or tree-climbing Zacheus. Or the Roman centurion with the ailing servant. Each of these, and many others (including those whose healing didn't make it into the record), were blessed by Jesus' willingness to set aside His agenda and address their needs. The same applied to those who came to Him with questions, like the rich young man or Nicodemus. In each case, His Spirit-led response was to act out of love and either heal a needy soul or respond to a question asked in sincerity.

He was ready to do so because of His limitless love for all, even when it entailed breaking cultural taboos and reaching out to people outside the Israelite nation. He spoke to a Samaritan woman about her multiple marriages and pointed her toward the living water He represented. (Jn.

---

[8] *The Interpreter's Bible*, vol. 7, 273.

4:4-26) Similarly, there was the Canaanite woman with the demon-possessed daughter, with whom He bantered about dogs and crumbs, and healed the daughter at a distance because of the mother's great faith. (Mt. 15:22-28)

~~~~~

We have before us, then, six areas in which Jesus was thoroughly prepared for His ministry. What is noteworthy about these areas is that they can serve as examples for us to follow. We are capable of improving our standing in at least five of these six areas, thus better preparing ourselves for whatever it is that God has called *us*. If they need improvement, we can strengthen our prayer life and our knowledge of Scripture. We can likewise be purposeful about increasing our resistance to temptation. If our circumstances and gifts permit, we can also be better equipped to share our faith with others, whether formally or informally.

And we can focus on heightening our sensitivity to the Spirit's leading, making us more alert to opportunities for service or encouragement that may come our way. In brief, Jesus' example offers us one area after another in which we can strive to be better prepared as His followers. Together, these approaches will enhance our overall relationship with God the Father, which was the first quality we ascribed to Jesus' preparation for His ministry.

There are other aspects of His life, however, which are beyond our human capacity. We are not divine and not imbued with the miraculous powers that Jesus had in treating sickness, raising the dead or otherwise showing His mastery of nature. Nor do we have the power, no matter how godly a life we have led, to meet with Moses and Elijah, or anyone else who died centuries before, while taking on a transfigured appearance that makes us dazzlingly white. All of these astonishing events in Jesus' life emerged from the three decades of preparation He had undergone, living a sinless life in Nazareth. The nature of that life and the start of His formal ministry began with John's baptism, an event that led to God speaking approvingly from a cloud.

Nor are Jesus' followers today advised to try walking on water or walking through walls. There was something profoundly different between Jesus and us, both before His resurrection and afterward, that enabled Him to transcend the normal laws of nature. No matter how much we try to prepare ourselves spiritually, the odds of us being able to copy Jesus' miraculous acts are infinitesimally small. Could God enable me in some crisis or other to walk on water or walk through a wall? Yes. Is that likely to happen? No. Instead, God expects us to prepare as best we can to act like His ambassadors in the situations we are much more likely to encounter, whether routine or extraordinary.

5: Prepare Ye the Way of the Lord

When a king was heading your way in biblical times, an advance team would go ahead and smooth the road as best they could. Maybe they'd do other things too, like cleaning up any roadside litter, sprucing up road signs that said "Jericho: 12 miles." These days, they'd ensure that all the gas station restrooms were meticulously clean and that all possible sniper positions had been noted and secured accordingly.

Regardless of what preparations were taken, the king's impending visit was taken seriously. The prophet Malachi says, "See, I will send my messenger, who will prepare the way before me." (Mal. 3:1) This announcement warns the Israelites that the king is coming to purify and judge, as later verses indicate; the messenger is giving you a heads up to get your act together. Isaiah has a similar admonition, which is cited in Matthew, Mark, and Luke's gospels. They each report John the Baptist as citing the prophet Isaiah: "Prepare the way for the Lord, make straight paths for him." (Mt. 3:3, Mk. 1:3 and Lk. 3:4)

What kind of preparation did John the Baptist have in mind? And more importantly, what preparation is expected of us today, if any? Hasn't the Lord already come, meaning we can dispense with this command? Or does it have another application for us today, so that we should be like the five wise bridesmaids and be prepared at all times for Jesus' second coming?

Let's begin with John. His was a call to repentance. "Get right with God," was his message, "because God is coming; prepare for His arrival." Get your spiritual house ready, he was saying. In reality, John is describing a two-way road construction or improvement project: preparing the road for the king but also preparing his hearers to receive the monarch on his arrival. How will you do that?

Imagine that two Secret Service agents came to your door and said, "The President will stop by your home tomorrow morning while he visits your town." The reason? "He wants to chat to ordinary voters like you about the upcoming primary, so we need to check your house and make sure everything's secure for his visit." After you've recovered from your shock, and after they've determined your home contains no potential threats to the President, you get to work. You vacuum every carpet in the house (twice, just to be sure). You put clean sheets on the bed. Who knows, maybe he'll want to take a nap. Unlikely, but you want to be prepared.

You clean the dishes. You line up whatever possible beverages you imagine the President or his entourage might want. You clean the bathroom (twice), hide all the clutter that's accumulated around the living room — stuffing some of it into the roll-top desk (surely he won't open that, will he?). Then you consider the outside. Got to mow the lawn. "Should I paint the front door?" which looks a tad faded? No time. By 11:30 tonight you're exhausted. You sleep on the sofa; you don't want to mess up the bed...

Did I say the Secret Service alerted you to the visit? Sorry, I meant to say the angel Gabriel. He said, "Just to give you a heads up, Jesus will stop by for a visit tomorrow morning. Some time between 10 and 11. No need for a security check; He knows all about you. Bye."

What will you do? Will you go into busy-ness overdrive, like Martha when she hosted Jesus? (Lk. 10:38-42) Will you anxiously Google Middle Eastern recipes in the hope that Jesus may like what you prepare? You'll certainly get some dates and olives. ("Does He prefer black or green? Better get both.")

We'll look more closely at Martha's focus on preparation in Chapter 34. For now, though, let's state the obvious: Jesus will be far more interested in you and your relationship with God than with your choice of olives. So a better question is, "How will you prepare *spiritually* for His arrival?"

What can you do to ease His journey or "make His path straight" to your home tomorrow morning? Nothing, really. The focus of your efforts clearly needs to be *you*, preparing a way to your heart, a heart that will greet Him with love, not fear; gladness, not trepidation; and absolute openness and honesty, not guile.

We know that all of us have immediate access to God in prayer, and that we can "boldly approach His throne of grace," (Heb. 4:16) just as we are with all our faults. But imagine for a moment that to be admitted to Jesus' presence tomorrow you first need to get past His TSA checkpoint. (His angels will set this up in your living room, Gabriel tells you.)

So picture yourself approaching the checkpoint staffed by a team of uniformed angels, all cheerfully telling you what you can't carry any further. "No pride, please; be sure to leave all your pride in the discard bins. And no hypocrisy. Can't take that in either. Anger, lust, fear — all of it must go. No doubts either please. All in the bins, please." (They're super-polite, these angels.)

As you approach the scanner, wondering if it'll pick up anything. "I'm not fearful," you tell yourself. "I threw fear in the pre-scanner bin. But what else might it detect...?"

Thus the all-important question, "How *will* you prepare for that face-to-face encounter with Jesus?" In reality, He doesn't need the road to be made straight; He will find His way to your door regardless of road conditions. And once He arrives, you'll almost certainly stop fretting about the olives.

PART 2: Getting Ready

6: How Do We Attain Readiness?

Don Murray said that "Professional writers never learn to write; they continue to learn writing all their professional lives."[9] He knew what he was talking about, as one of those rare people who was both a superb writer (and Pulitzer Prize winner) and a superb teacher — "perhaps the most influential writing teacher in the nation's history." That was the view of another legendary writing teacher, Roy Peter Clark.[10]

One can easily adapt his comment on writing to the Christian's quest for readiness. In discipleship too, we never finally and fully arrive; we are learning all our lives how to follow Jesus and how to improve our state of spiritual readiness. As we saw in Chapter 4, we can identify six qualities in Jesus' life that we can and should emulate. By way of review, these are:

- His close walk with and dependence on His heavenly Father
- His vigorous prayer life
- His knowledge of Scripture
- His uncompromising resistance of temptation
- His teaching and mentoring ministry, preparing His disciples to spread the gospel after He left them, and
- His openness to Spirit-guided spontaneity.

How are we to combine these into a unified approach to enhancing our spiritual readiness to live out God's will? Three metaphors will help as we consider the heart of readiness. They speak to three types of preparedness: readiness for the unexpected; readiness for specific challenges known in advance; and readiness for living a godly life in general.

First, let us consider members of an army's Special Forces unit. These are individuals who have undergone rigorous selection and were vetted for their physical and mental fitness. Next came extensive and intense training to get them combat-ready for the widest imaginable array of military operations. Then, in addition, there may be operation-focused training as well, as they prepare for a particular mission. Think for example of the Israeli forces that practiced for the raid on the Entebbe

---

[9] Don Murray: *Writing for Your Readers*, 1.
[10] https://www.poynter.org/archive/2006/the-take-and-the-give-a-tribute-to-don-murray/. Accessed April 18,2024.

airport in Uganda, to rescue passengers and crew on an Air France airliner hijacked in June 1976.[11] Or consider the US Navy Seals who captured Osama bin Laden in Pakistan in May 2011.[12] This group of elite special forces likewise was able to practice for their raid, conducted under the cover of great secrecy.

While these and other special operations are unique in their settings and demands, one thing that is common to all of them is the readiness of the participants to undertake high-risk missions—thanks to endless training and a clear sense of their mission.[13]

Christians likewise need to be at the ready at all times for an unexpected task God may have in mind for them. As Oswald Chambers puts it, "Be ready for the sudden surprise visits of God. A ready person never needs to get ready."[14]

A second metaphor worth considering is studying for some major qualifying exam. If you are an aspiring lawyer, for instance, you will spend hours preparing for the bar exam in the state where you want to practice, in addition to the years you spent in law school learning everything from criminal procedure to tort law. Unlike the type of "surprise assignment" just mentioned, this preparation is one you've worked on long and hard, as you knew the date of the exam well in advance.

Likewise for Christians, you know some tough challenges are going to come your way in life for which you can prepare in advance. An obvious parallel is if you're studying for the ministry and after completing your academic training you need to prepare for your church's ordination exam. Or it could well be that bar exam, an essential step to fulfill what you believe is your calling to serve as a public defender in your community. Or the completion of your nursing program, to honor God's call to serve in that arena.

The parallel here is that long preparation may be needed to fully live out your Christian identity, in response to what you believe is God's leading in your life. It's important to recognize too that starting out thinking you're called to serve as a public defender may not match where you end up. It could be that along the way God-sent opportunities arise and you end up practicing family law instead. Law school proved to be an

---

[11] See https://en.wikipedia.org/wiki/Entebbe_raid for more information. Accessed Sept. 5, 2023.

[12] https://www.military.com/history/osama-bin-laden-operation-neptune-spear. Accessed Sept. 5, 2023.

[13] William McRaven, who oversaw the bin Laden raid, has analyzed eight special operations in his book *Spec Ops*. One of the qualities he says characterize successful operations, and to which he refers repeatedly, is purpose.

[14] Oswald Chambers: *My Utmost for His Highest*, April 18.

essential time of preparation, as did the bar exam. But it wasn't the final step in shaping your calling.

The third metaphor to explore is that of spiritual maturity. The parallel here is that of maturity in general. We don't expect to see a grown woman bursting into tears on aisle seven in the supermarket because she can't find the right kind of dental floss. Nor would we expect her husband to throw a level-ten tantrum at the dry cleaner's because his jacket wasn't ready when promised.

Mature adults, we expect, show the following qualities, among others. They
- Accept responsibility
- Accept their limitations
- Control their emotions, displaying emotions proportionate to the situation
- Behave appropriately given the circumstances
- Are humble, in that they have a proper estimation of themselves
- Are realists
- Handle failure or disappointment without having to kick the dog or going into a sulk, and
- Have firm convictions but are open to carefully considered change.

You can undoubtedly think of other qualities. Or, if you see wisdom and maturity as two sides of the same coin, you might embrace the words of novelist Louise Penny, whose character Inspector Gamache says: "There are four things that lead to wisdom. They are four sentences we learn to say, and mean. 'I don't know. I need help. I'm sorry. I was wrong.'"[15]

However you choose to define maturity in general, you will soon see a comparable set of qualities that ought to characterize the mature Christian. Ideally, we ought always to be displaying what Paul calls the fruits of the Spirit in every aspect of our lives. He lists these as "love, joy, peace, forbearance, kindness, goodness, faithfulness, gentleness and self-control." (Gal. 5:22-23)

It is difficult to imagine that emotional outburst on aisle seven or the temper tantrum over the jacket coming from someone whose Spirit-filled disposition is marked by the qualities Paul identified. Imagine for a moment that the nine qualities Paul lists were aspects on which we'd be judged in the Spiritual Olympics. How would the judges score us on each of these? Unlike the legendary Romanian gymnast Nadia Comaneci, who scored an unprecedented perfect ten in the 1976 Olympics, we'd no doubt

---

[15] This advice appears in several of Louise Penny's novels. See her website's FAQ: https://www.louisepenny.com/faqs.htm. Accessed April 18, 2024.

fall short of perfection.

But that's not why Paul lists these nine qualities. Rather, they are aspirational, areas in which we should heighten our spiritual "skill set," and thus enhance our overall readiness to serve and witness as Christians wherever God has placed us.

7: God's Response to Readiness

We're entering dangerous territory here. Think of Peter trying to "correct" Jesus' statement about His impending death, after which "Jesus turned and said to Peter, 'Get behind me, Satan!'" (Mt. 16:23) Or in Acts when Peter is commanded in his vision to eat, and he says, "Surely not, Lord!" (Acts 10:14)

Contradicting a direct command from God is never wise. Nor is thinking we can compel God to act in a certain way. Yet there are instances when, in a sense, we can do just that. We can, with due humility, call on a trustworthy God to deliver on His promises. For example, "God has said, 'Never will I leave you; never will I forsake you.'" (Heb. 13:5)

Then there's the daring claim made by Meister Eckhart (1260-1328), a German theologian and mystic: "... finding thee ready He [God] is obliged to act, to overflow into thee; just as the sun must needs burst forth when the air is bright and clear, and is unable to contain itself."[16] In other words, if we are ready to serve God, God in turn *must of necessity* respond and empower us for what He wants us to do. The notion that we can at times *oblige* God to act is astonishing.

Maybe this sounds uncomfortably upside down, with us telling God what to do rather than the other way round. An easier-to-accept notion may be the idea of partnering with God, when He sees that you're ready, awake (like those bridesmaids), and eager to follow Him. But don't lose sight of the words, "...*finding thee ready.*"

---

[16] Quoted in Gordon S. Jackson: *The God Who Blesses*, 95.

8: Preparing with Patience

*She seems to me to be full of good will, but she would go faster than grace.
One does not become holy all at once.*

— Brother Lawrence[17]

What can Brother Lawrence mean by "faster than grace"? Probably just this: As children and teens, we grow at a certain rate; we can't artificially rush things. It's the same with spiritual growth and readiness. We can't grow faster than God has in mind for us.

Eugene Peterson wrote a book titled *A Long Obedience in the Same Direction*. That concept sums up rather well the nature of Christian discipleship. When Paul used the metaphor of the Christian life being like running a race, he was not thinking of a sprint. Rather, Christians are in it for the duration, the spiritual equivalent of a half-marathon, maybe even a full one.

Each element in Peterson's book title is worth noting. Acquiring readiness, and the holiness on which it is built, takes time; it's a *long* process. One doesn't become holy by adding water and microwaving for two minutes. The process also requires the *obedience* to which Peterson refers, and it's a long obedience. Finally, holiness demands a steady walk *in the same direction*. No veering to the left or the right.

Steadily, though, our growth and maturation expand our capacity for readiness. In human terms, we can do more for God's Kingdom as a twenty-year-old than when we were two. As we grow, our readiness heightens; we are better prepared for service.

Following his dramatic conversion, the Apostle Paul may well have wanted to jump in right away to start his ministry to the Gentiles. Yet we read that he went off to Arabia and later returned to Damascus, where he had encountered the risen Christ. Then, after three years he went to Jerusalem.[18] We don't know if he spent all three years in Arabia; Scripture isn't clear on that. But it's reasonable to infer that he spent much of this time in prayer, reflection and other kinds of preparation for his subsequent ministry before meeting Peter in Jerusalem—and presumably launching his massively important ministry to the Gentiles. Three years' preparation: that was long enough to get a graduate degree or two, and a

---

[17] Brother Lawrence: *The Practice of the Presence of God*, ninth letter.
[18] Gal. 1:15-18.

delay that must have demanded great patience from a man just itching to spread the good news of the gospel.

During our own Christian walk we may be called upon to display exceptional patience as we await clarity on the work He has for us en route. As Matthew Henry put it, "Sometimes it is long before God calls His servants out to the work which of old He designed them for, and has been graciously preparing them for."[19]

---

[19] Matthew Henry: *One-Volume Commentary on the Bible*, 74.

9: Time in the Desert

Deserts have long had a special place in Scripture and in how Christians have used them as a metaphor for their faith journeys. They convey a sense of isolation and hardship, where our senses are intensified and our capacity to hear God's voice is heightened.

Jesus began His ministry by spending forty days in the desert, clarifying His mission and resisting the most intense temptation to compromise what His Father had called Him to do. Nor was it a coincidence that He was following in the footsteps of Moses, who traded the luxury of Pharaoh's court for the harshness of the desert—the kind of territory through which, not coincidentally, he would later lead the children of Israel to the Promised Land. John the Baptist likewise located himself in the desert, living a harsh and spartan life, as he paved the way for Jesus' ministry.

Sometimes, as with John and Jesus, going to the desert is a voluntary matter. Moses, by contrast, had little choice, fleeing as a fugitive after murdering an Egyptian overseer. But regardless of what drives us there, deserts can be important places of instruction and preparation, incubators that strengthen us and prepare us for a task ahead. Their quietness and separation from the bustle of urban life allows us better to concentrate on God and hear His word to us.

A desert experience can be a bleak time, which we wish would end soon. At times God may send us into a figurative desert for a specific reason—or, a literal desert, as with Philip and his encounter with the eunuch. (Acts 8) As Matthew Henry notes, "He [Philip] would never have thought of going thither, into a desert; small probability of finding work there! Yet thither he is sent. Sometimes God opens a door of opportunity to His ministers in places very unlikely."[20] Opportunity, yes, and for preparation too.

---

[20] Matthew Henry *One-Volume Commentary on the Bible*, 1,667.

10: The Perfect Instrument

St. Ignatius of Loyola (1491-1556) was a Spanish priest who founded the Jesuit movement, famous for its missionary and educational work. The Jesuit movement played an important part in the Catholic counter-reformation. Included in Ignatius' legacy is a Latin phrase worthy of our attention. He described the ideal Jesuit as an *instrumentum conjunctum cum Deo*, "an instrument shaped to the hand of God." In other words, someone who was "a perfect fit" for God's hand.

It would be presumptuous for any one of us to think we've matured spiritually to the point where we're a perfect tool in the hand of God. Like Ignatius, however, we do well to see this as an ideal standard to attain, submitting ourselves to God's shaping and refining as we steadily work toward perfection as a tool in the Lord's work.

What remains in your life as a barrier to that perfect fit? What does God still need to do in your life to shape the tool that you are? To be sure, you're already of great use in Kingdom work. But what rough edges need smoothing out to improve God's grip? Or what needs sharpening so that you can better do the cutting God needs?

To some degree, we are all ready to serve His purposes. We would do well, however, to bear in mind C. S. Lewis' words: "We should be pleased with our progress, but never satisfied."[21] You are ready, then; but you could be "readier."

---

[21] An extensive search has failed to produce the source of this Lewis quote.

PART 3: Living Out Our Readiness

11: Coming in on What's Happening

Eugene Peterson is best known for his paraphrase of the Bible, known as *The Message*. Less well known is that he was a Presbyterian pastor for twenty-nine years and a prolific writer. In one of his more than thirty books arising from his experience he describes the context in which he goes about his pastoral duties:

In every visit, every meeting I attend, every appointment I keep, I have been anticipated. The risen Christ got there ahead of me. The risen Christ is in that room already. What is He doing? What is He saying? What is going on?

In order to fix the implications of that text in my vocation, I have taken to quoting it before every visit or meeting: 'He is risen... He is going before you to 1020 Emmorton Road; there you will see Him, as He told you.' Later in the day it will be, 'He is risen... He is going before you to St. Joseph's Hospital; there you will see Him, as He told you.'"[22]

What does your day look like? What is your equivalent of 1020 Emmorton Road or St. Joseph's Hospital? Peterson continues:

We are always coming in on something that is already going on…. [A]lways we are dealing with what the risen Christ has already set in motion, already brought into being.

That classroom or office you will enter later today, then, or the construction site or assembly plant—remember that the risen Christ has been there ahead of you. The Holy Spirit has been at work in people's lives, in some cases preparing them to be open to whatever you can bring them this day. But you too have been well prepared for this day and its tasks. With God's help, you will be ready for whatever the day demands. In His grace, you may discover that you're even better prepared than you thought: He's done much of the groundwork for you.

We need to be careful, though, not to demand that this groundwork be perfect or complete in every respect. Dawson Trotman, founder of The Navigators, a Bible reading ministry, "was not big on having the circumstances just right. He encouraged Christians to move as soon as there was an opportunity. For a swimmer who is getting ready to swim laps, rather than waiting until the water is at the perfect temperature and the waves have settled, Trotman would suggest that the swimmer jump

---

[22] Eugene H. Peterson: *Living the Message*, Sept. 18.

in as soon as the water is available."[23]

Things are already in motion; time to join in. Or jump in…

---

[23] Ken Albert, Susan Fletcher and Doug Hankins: *Dawson Trotman: In His Own Words*, 56.

12: "For Such a Time as This" — A Risk-Filled Readiness

... who knows but that you have come to your royal position for such a time as this?

— Esther 4:14

When Fidel Castro was still prime minister of Cuba, a Presbyterian woman living under the tight restrictions of this Communist government undertook a speaking tour in the United States. In one church she emphasized how she believed that God had not placed her and other Christians in their country by mistake, and that He had a clear purpose for them being where they were at that difficult time.

As the saying goes, "Everybody's gotta be some place." Christians, though, accept that they are in places assigned by God, not by chance. Which brings us to the remarkable story of Esther. She is the Jewish woman thrust into the highest levels of the Persian kingdom, becoming the queen of Ahasuerus, also known as Xerxes. She is chosen to replace the deposed Queen Vashti, who offended the king by refusing his summons to appear before him. Not a smart move when you're married to a dictator. It isn't clear what was behind her refusal.

The book that bears Esther's name raises other questions too. For one thing, we are prompted to ask why this is the only book in the Bible that does not mention or refer directly to God. Then there's the odd incident of Mordecai, Esther's guardian. He insults Haman, a high-ranking official, by not bowing to him: "Mordecai would not kneel down or pay him honor." (Est. 3:2) The expectation that he would do so was normal courtesy, to recognize Haman's rank; this was not a matter of worshiping the man. So the reason for Mordecai's refusal remains a puzzle. The point is that Haman is so insulted that he begins to plot the death not only of Mordecai but all the Jews.

We could spend much time exploring the intrigues of the court, the motivations of the various players, and the hatred Haman has for the Jews. Instead, our interest is with Queen Esther herself. After a year's preparation, when she is primped and preened by her own team of beauticians, she is presented to the king. He is wowed by her beauty and charm, and we have the fairytale ending when she is chosen to be his queen.

But wait: that's *not* the ending. In fact, it's just the prelude to the heart of the story, which entails the existential threat from Haman to kill all the Jews. This is followed by Mordecai's pitch to Esther to use her position to approach the king and avoid this calamity. And that is where the best-known verse in this book appears, when Mordecai says: "… who knows but that you have come to your royal position for such a time as this?" (Est. 4:14) In other words, even though God isn't mentioned in any of the dialog between them, or anywhere else in the book, its central message is that God is in charge. Esther has benefited from all the beauty preparation the palace could provide her. But more significant is that the chain of events that led to her ascent to the throne was no coincidence; God was behind it all. The unfolding of events wasn't a mere string of coincidences, with Esther just happening to be in the right place at the right time and in the right clothes. God's fingerprints were all over these events, even if His hand wasn't visible.

We have a similar pattern of events in the story of Joseph. In hindsight, he sees God's plan and with remarkable magnanimity he assures his brothers that he bears them no malice: "[Do] not be distressed and do not be angry with yourselves for selling me here, because it was to save lives that God sent me ahead of you." (Gen. 45:5)

Esther then prepares herself with fasting and prayer for three days. She urges the rest of the Jews to do likewise. Then, at great risk she approaches the king without being summoned. If he were having a bad hair day or for no reason at all, he could have her deposed or executed for such a breach of protocol. But no, he hears her out and we see karma played out in the next several chapters as the tables are turned and Haman ends up on the gallows he has erected, not Mordecai. The story is masterfully told, with irony and twists that would do justice to a made-for-Netflix thriller. But while we already know the ending, we need to reflect a moment more on Esther's part in the story.

We've already mentioned the physical preparation she underwent to enhance her God-given beauty. We need to note too her spiritual preparation, which no doubt began long before her arrival at the palace. Having been brought up as a Jew, she was steeped in the knowledge of Yahweh's power to save. The story of the Exodus and God's care for His people would have been foremost in her mind as she faced this crisis.

Mordecai says, in the first half of verse 14, "if you remain silent at this time, relief and deliverance for the Jews will arise from another place." We can't be sure what this cryptic remark means. But while he's putting his hopes in Esther and her courage to approach the king, he seems to be saying that you're not indispensable in God's plans. If you don't take advantage of the situation in which He has placed you, He will find another way to rescue His people. Mordecai's comment reflects a deep faith in God's capacity to save yet at the same time he is almost bullying her into acting.

Whatever Mordecai's true motive, he was stating an important truth that applies universally to God's people: In whatever place we find ourselves right now, *this* is where God has placed us. It is *here* we are ready to serve today. And it is *here*, if necessary, where we are to act in a time of great need or crisis. Jean-Pierre de Caussade said, "The whole essence of the spiritual life consists in recognizing the designs of God for us for *the present moment*."[24] (Emphasis added.)

For Esther, the "present moment" meant she had two options. She could choose passivity and hope that, despite Mordecai's prediction that she too would be swept up in the slaughter of the Jews, her Jewish identity might remain secret and that her life would be spared. Or she could choose the high-risk path of approaching the king unannounced, to set in motion the events that would trap Haman – and spare the Jews. Much could go wrong, as she was well aware. As she told Mordecai, "If I perish, I perish." (Est. 4:16)

She exemplified perfectly what G. K. Chesterton wrote some 2,500 years later: "Courage is almost a contradiction in terms. It means a strong desire to live taking the form of a readiness to die."[25] Her courage prevailed as she proved to be the right person in the right place at the right time. She lived out her readiness, well aware that it was for such a time that God had brought her to this unexpected position of influence in the Persian court.

But that merging of time and place and task may not be your experience right now. It may be that you can in all honesty say that your present location is a barren land. You may be convinced that God has little or no use for you here. Maybe. Maybe you are hearing a call to move elsewhere, for which your present location has been a training ground to equip you for what lies ahead. Or perhaps you're tired, bored or frightened and however you rationalize it, you want to turn your back on God's work in this place. Whether it's time to move to another arena of service, that's for you to figure out, with God's help. For now, though, your current location is where you are to live out your faith.

Two final thoughts, first from Warren Wiersbe: "If our service for the Lord doesn't make us grow, two things may be true: either we're in the wrong place, or we have the wrong attitude toward the right place."[26]

Second, the insight from Oswald Chambers: "Never allow the

---

[24] https://www.firstthings.com/article/1998/02/the-school-of-sanctification. Accessed April 18, 2024.
[25] https://www.chesterton.org/quotations/courage/. Accessed April 18, 2024.
[26] Warren Wiersbe: *On Being a Servant of God.*

thought, 'I am of no use where I am.' You certainly can be of no use where you are not."[27]

---

[27] Oswald Chambers: *My Utmost for His Highest*, Oct. 17.

13: Ripeness vs. Unripeness

I was studying Spanish in Guatemala in 1992, during yet another season of political instability in that country's seemingly perpetual struggle for democratic rule. One of my teachers, eager for a more just social order, said that the climate wasn't yet ripe enough for change. Things were still "too green," as he put it. Sadly, more than three decades later, that beautiful but beleaguered country still hasn't attained the stability of which my teacher dreamed. Perhaps conditions remain "too green."

This concept of ripeness vs unripeness has a twofold application for our purposes: to the people or circumstances that need to move closer to God's preferred state, and to us — who might similarly need growth and ripening. Are there areas in our lives that resist ripening to bear the fruit that God expects of us? How do we rate when we reflect on Paul's list, which we initially cited in Chapter 6: "[T]he fruit of the Spirit is love, joy, peace, forbearance, kindness, goodness, faithfulness, gentleness and self-control…"? (Gal. 5:22)

And what about others whose lives we seek to influence, either mentoring them in their faith or aspiring to introduce them to the saving knowledge of the gospel? James S. Stewart, a Scottish pastor and author, said that pastors should remind themselves of the opportunity facing them each Sunday morning: "God is to be in action today, through me, for these people; this day may be crucial, this service decisive, for someone now ripe for the vision of Jesus."[28]

Or it may be a longer-term quest in which Christians are engaged. William Wilberforce, for example, is well known as an English politician and Christian voice against slavery. He was instrumental in ending Britain's slave trade, but it took decades of lobbying and campaigning until he and his fellow abolitionists could change the country's mood.

On a more individual note involving Britain's slave trade, John Newton's discovery of "Amazing Grace," the hymn for which he rightly became famous, did not immediately end his role as a captain of a slave trading ship. One of his biographers said it took about twenty-five years before he saw that he was complicit in this evil and finally turned his back on slavery. A long time, in other words, for fruit to ripen in his life and

---

[28] Quoted in J. Doberstein: *Minister's Prayer Book*, 398.

attain a level of readiness befitting a more mature faith.[29]

Therefore, in addition to monitoring our own spiritual weaknesses and gaps, we ought also to be paying attention to the environment in which we live. We might be able to discern opportunities for "mending the earth" that weren't there yesterday or the day before. We're referring here to the Hebrew concept of *tikkun olam*. The concept has undergone change over the years, but its current meaning refers "to the pursuit of social justice or 'the establishment of godly qualities throughout the world,' based on the idea that 'Jews bear responsibility not only for their own moral, spiritual and material welfare, but also for the welfare of society at large.'"[30] Those values are certainly compatible with Christian views.

So, we are engaged in a two-fold mission. We are to seek those conditions that will ripen the spiritual fruit we are already equipped to produce. (We might want to consider what "spiritual greenhouse" conditions would encourage that process for us?) But we are also to keep our eye on our environment, on people and possibilities for societal change as well. In this regard, we should heed Yale Kneeland's counsel: "Wait for your cues and give them your full attention."[31]

---

[29] Jonathan Aitkin: *John Newton: From Disgrace to Amazing Grace*, 112.
[30] https://en.wikipedia.org/wiki/Tikkun_olam. Accessed Sept. 5, 2023.
[31] Quoted in Gordon S. Jackson: *Never Scratch a Tiger with a Short Stick*, 99.

14: Ready for Communion

Picture the scene. You're a lay person, helping serve Communion, the Lord's Supper, or the Eucharist in your church on Sunday, however your tradition describes it. Worshippers have formed a line, or they're kneeling at the rail. Many of the people you serve are familiar; some you greet by name. "Edward, the body of Christ, broken for you, Larissa, the blood of Christ, shed for you...."

Out of the corner of your eye you notice who's coming up soon. He's not the next, but the one after; he's not a regular at church but he looks familiar. Then you're serving the person immediately in front of him: "Carly, the body of Christ, broken for you..."

That's when it hits you: he's the lawyer representing your spouse in a bitter divorce. You met him for the first time this week, having previously dealt with him only over the phone and via email. The meeting did not go well. In fact, it reached what in retrospect were embarrassingly heated levels. You thought he was a slimy, conniving, money-grabbing bastard. You told him so. His sneering retort merely fueled your anger and reinforced your disdain for the man. Afterwards, you wondered — only briefly — if you had overreacted and owed him an apology. But no, he had been genuinely deceptive and, you remain convinced, deserving of your wrath.

Or maybe it was a case of road rage, after which you furiously exchanged words, or an angry and irrational customer you had to deal with. Or maybe it was another mom who was hosting the playgroup who yet again let your son be bullied by one of the older boys.

Now the person's in front of you. With hands already outstretched for you to serve the elements, eye contact is made, followed by immediate recognition...

You remember the gist of Jesus' words: "Therefore, if you are offering your gift at the altar and there remember that your brother or sister has something against you, leave your gift there in front of the altar. First go and be reconciled to them; then come and offer your gift." (Mt. 5:23-24)

Too late. Now, you ask yourself, was there anything you should have, or could have, done to be ready for this moment?

15: Preparing for Failure

One of Christianity's most common cliches is that we are called to be faithful, not successful. We are to leave success (however we define it) to God alone. While that's a comforting sentiment at one level, the reality is that nobody welcomes failure, not even Christians. Yet that's something for which we need to prepare. Things don't always work out the way we would like. Nor do they work out in the way we think God would prefer.

Let us look briefly at what we could see as a drama in three acts. It concerns the example of William Borden, an exceptionally gifted young man from a wealthy Chicago family who forsook a promising secular career to become a missionary. He died unexpectedly of cerebral meningitis in 1913 at the age of twenty-five, while in Egypt. He had already established such a strong reputation as an exemplary and sacrificial Christian that his death received national coverage in the United States. Papers typically mourned his death as a waste. That was Act 1.

Act 2 was the publication, in 1926, of his biography, titled "Borden of Yale."[32] It described a life of profound commitment to Christ and the self-sacrifice he undertook.

Act 3 comes years later, with the arrival on the scene of a Wheaton College student, Ken Taylor. He came across the Borden biography and was shattered by what he saw as a sheer waste of a life. *Christianity Today's* obituary of Taylor said the young student "deliberately turned his back on God. Then, he reflects, God 'reached out and grabbed me and pulled me back.' Deeply contrite, he surrendered his life to any and all spheres of Christian service."[33]

And why, you might ask, was *Christianity Today* even doing an obituary on Ken Taylor, who died in 2005 at age eighty-eight? It was because his paraphrase of the Bible, *The Living Bible*, was a spectacularly successful publishing venture: it sold forty million copies, bringing the word of God to millions in an easy to follow, contemporary English.

Taylor was emphatic that reading *Borden of Yale* was the pivotal point in his Christian journey. He said, "This book changed the course of my life. Spiritually speaking, had it not been for this book, my life would have

---

[32] Mrs. William Howard: *Borden of Yale.*
[33] https://www.christianitytoday.com/ct/2005/juneweb-only/55.0a.html. Accessed Sept. 21, 2023.

been a spiritual shambles."[34] And *The Living Bible* would never have existed. What seemed like a tragic waste of a young life in 1913 was later a critical element in spreading God's word to infinitely more people than William Borden would likely have reached in a missionary career. God's seemingly convoluted plan, in other words, wasn't grounded in failure or waste after all. US poet Edwin Markham would have understood our three-act drama. He wrote: "Defeat may serve as well as victory to shake the soul and let the glory out."[35]

So how does the story of Borden and Taylor instruct us about readiness or preparation? Two points. First, we ought to expect and anticipate what others may see as failure. Twenty years in the mission field without apparent success. A promising academic career cut short by drug addiction. Losing the state soccer championship because of an own goal you scored... You can look to your own experiences for more examples of what you see as failures. They can be life-changing or more modest, like the example of Jesus' disciples' abortive fishing venture:

> *When [Jesus] had finished speaking, he said to Simon, "Put out into deep water, and let down the nets for a catch." Simon answered, "Master, we've worked hard all night and haven't caught anything. But because you say so, I will let down the nets." When they had done so, they caught such a large number of fish that their nets began to break. So they signaled their partners in the other boat to come and help them, and they came and filled both boats so full that they began to sink.* (Lk. 5:4-7)

This is a simple example of Jesus transforming a failed fishing expedition into bountiful success. Many of His miracles could be seen the same way. A catering failure in Cana sees water transformed into wine; a failure of the medical system that leads a desperate woman with a hemorrhage to touch Jesus' robe; or the failure of Jesus to arrive in time to heal Lazarus that leads to his death. In each case, though, the failure isn't the end of the story.

And that is our second point. God's sovereign plan and purpose trumps everything.

As Paul assures the Romans, "[W]e know that in all things God works for the good of those who love him, who have been called according to his purpose." (Rom. 8:28)

Our overall readiness to serve our Lord must make provision for things to go wrong, for disappointment. At the same time, though, we

---

[34] https://www.librarycat.org/lib/whbclibrary/item/226449150. Cited April 18, 2024.
[35] Quoted in Gordon S. Jackson, *Never Scratch a Tiger with a Short Stick*, 70.

must build in a resilience that assures us that in Kingdom work, "...nothing is wasted or incomplete," as the *New Zealand Prayer Book* puts it.[36] What may seem like a failure may therefore, in the long run, prove to be what we could call a blessing in disguise. Unless we have a clear indication to quit, perseverance is needed. The counsel of Matthew Henry is apposite: "We must not abruptly quit the callings wherein we are called because we have not the success in them we promised ourselves... The ministers of the gospel must continue to let down that net, though they have perhaps toiled long and caught nothing."[37]

---

[36] *New Zealand Prayer Book*: 856.
[37] Matthew Henry: *One-Volume Commentary on the Bible*, 1,428.

16: Just Wake Up! — Readiness Delayed

Jennie Litvick was an accomplished player of the shofar, the ram's horn sounded at various Jewish festivals that have their roots in the Old Testament. The teruah is one of those shofar calls, consisting of a series of nine staccato blasts. That was one of Litvick's favorite calls, which was like an alarm clock, she would say, to "summon the listener, 'Wake up, wake up, wake up. Now is the time to do something.'"[38]

At times we Christians may need the equivalent of a Jennie Litvick in our lives, to blast us into action with the call, "Wake up, wake up. Now is the time to do something!"

Maybe we are chronic procrastinators, putting off the important while attending to more welcome, easier, or more gratifying tasks. Oh, we say we're ready enough to tackle what we know deep down are the more important "to-do" items. But are we in the meantime quietly sleeping our way through an obvious opportunity or need that God has presented us? Especially if we're "sleeping the sleep of the dead," Paul has a word for us, quoting a fragment of unknown origin but possibly from an early hymn: "…it is said: 'Wake up, sleeper, rise from the dead, and Christ will shine on you.' Be very careful, then, how you live—not as unwise but as wise, making the most of every opportunity…'" (Eph. 5:14-16)

If we're honest, most of the time our problem isn't trying to discover God's will, it's *doing* it. Beyond that, there's not much to be said. We could spend time looking at various reasons why we don't do what we know God has called us to or otherwise expects of us, whether it concerns a general or specific will for our lives. We could look at the nature of the temptations we face and why we succumb to them; we could reflect on our lack of courage or on our predisposition to choose a sinful path rather than a holy one. But none of this takes us beyond the fundamental point we already know: "This is the way; walk in it." (Is. 30:21)

We are already ready. Nothing more is needed.

---

[38] Litvick's obituary in *The Economist*, July 19, 2019.

17: Ready to Forgive

On October 2, 2006, Charles Carl Roberts IV "carried his guns and his rage into an Amish schoolhouse near Nickel Mines, Pennsylvania. Five schoolgirls died that day, and five others were seriously wounded."[39] Roberts then took his own life. The attack drew massive national and international media attention, for two reasons.

The first was the sheer horror of the event, and especially the incongruity of a community known for its placid faith being shattered by murderous gunfire. The second, as Donald Kraybill and his fellow authors point out in their analysis of this event, was the inability of those outside this small Amish community to grasp how they could instantly reach out to Roberts' family in forgiveness. The media, and the outside world generally, could not understand how this community was able immediately to segue into forgiveness mode after the shooting, without revealing even any impulse to seek revenge. As Kraybill and his co-authors write, "[T]he biggest surprise at Nickel Mines was not the intrusion of evil but the Amish response. The biggest surprise was Amish grace."[40]

The writers conclude this moving study of the Nickel Mines attack with a crucial observation: The Amish commitment to forgiveness is integral to their Christian ethos. This commitment "is not a small patch tacked onto their fabric of faithfulness. Rather, their commitment to forgive is intricately woven into their lives and their communities… For them, forgiveness is more than a good thing to do. It is absolutely central to their Christian faith."

Their capacity for forgiveness, they explain, contrasts sharply with the predominant US culture, which "nourishes revenge and mocks grace." What the Amish teach us instead "is that how we choose to move on from tragic injustice is culturally formed." Perhaps no Christian community has better modeled how to forgive than the Amish, who have systematically cultivated this quality over their 500-year history.

Tragically, dozens more mass shootings at places of worship have followed since this Pennsylvanian shooting, in the United States and

---

[39] These passages describing the Nickel Mines shooting are quoted in Gordon S. Jackson, *Christians, Free Expression and the Common Good*, 167.

elsewhere. It is difficult to think of a greater horror inflicted on a church community than such violence. But if such an event occurred at your church, how ready do you think your fellow believers, and you personally, would be to follow this Amish example of forgiveness? On our own, and humanly speaking, this seems like an impossibility. The Amish, however, are a tight-knit community, and therein lies their secret: What you and I would find immensely difficult to do as individuals we might be far more ready to undertake as members of a similar community — one that stands ready to forgive even the most horrific wrongs.

The Amish, of all people, have honored Jesus' expectation that emerges from his encounter with Peter, who asked how many times he should forgive. Is it seven? Rabbinic teaching was that one should forgive one's brother three times. So Peter is probably trying to impress Jesus by doubling that number and adding yet another "forgiveness" just to be sure. Yet Jesus' answer of "until seventy times seven" (Mt. 18:22)[41] is His way of saying you've asked a question without an answer. "Forgive as many times as you need to," is the message. Jesus is not literally saying seventy-seven times,[42] after which you can stop forgiving. And we can imagine Him pointing to the Amish.

---

[41] This is the more familiar *The King James Version* wording.
[42] This is how the *NIV* translates this number. However, the significance remains the same.

18: Protecting Our Master Grace

Matthew Henry says that "Joshua was remarkable for his courage—it was his master grace, and yet it seems he had need to be again and again cautioned not to be afraid."[43] Read the first nine verses of Joshua 1 and you'll see for yourself. Three times in these verses God tells Moses' successor:
- "Be strong and courageous..." (verse 6)
- "Be strong and very courageous..." (verse 7) and a repeat:
- "Be strong and courageous..." (verse 9)

If this weren't enough, God repeats himself in verse 9, in negative form: "do not be discouraged..."

Finally, to remind Joshua yet again, the chapter concludes with the people themselves saying, "Only be strong and courageous!" (verse 18)

You can be sure that with this admonition drummed into his consciousness, he will almost certainly never have forgotten God's admonition during the turbulent times he subsequently faced. Few people in the Bible were more ready for the role to which God had called them than Joshua. His long apprenticeship under Moses, his experience in the desert, and his innate skills prepared him well. And as a bonus, as Matthew Henry points out, was this master grace of courage.

What about you? Is there a "master grace" people have said characterizes your Christian walk? Patience, perhaps? Or compassion? Or a special love for children? There's likely to be at least one aspect of your "readiness repertoire" that others have pointed out to you. And that's precisely the area that the Tempter has noticed as well.

Don't be surprised if this is precisely the area that the Tempter will target in your vulnerable moments. With due humility, consider identifying that one aspect of who you are that qualifies as your master grace. Pray for special strength that those around you may continue to see it today.

The late John Stott provided a useful way of thinking about temptation or, more accurately, a strategy for overcoming it, thus ensuring we remain in a state of perpetual readiness. He says we should establish an early-warning system. We need to put the sentries in place. For the

---

[43] Matthew Henry: *One-Volume Commentary on the Bible*, 227.

most part, we know our areas of weakness. Maybe we're especially prone to showing unwarranted anger. Or it may be the sin of gluttony or sexual temptation.

But we could be equally vulnerable in the area of our strength. Whether it is our weakness or strength, we're far more likely to resist the temptation if we've been proactive, and in effect put sentries in place to alert us to approaching temptation. Stott said, "The posting of sentries is a commonplace of *military* tactics; *moral* sentry-duty is equally indispensable. Are we so foolish as to allow the enemy to overwhelm us, simply because we have posted no sentries to warn us of his approach?"[44]

Imagine beginning each day by praying something like this: "Lord, You know my weaknesses and strengths even better than I do. Please post the sentries I need this day to stand guard over me, at the edge of the camp, to alert me when temptation is coming my way." Whether you want to see these sentries as a helpful mind-game or perhaps as angels looking out for you, you can be assured God will take your prayer seriously. And you can be further assured that God's sentries seconded to ensure your protection will, like the one who posted them, "neither slumber nor sleep." (Ps. 121:4)

---

[44] John Stott: *The Message of the Sermon on the Mount*, 90-91

19: Readiness and Two Kinds of Gifts

Have thy tools ready; God will find thee work.

— *Charles Kingsley*[45]

Imagine you're a plumber, pest exterminator or firefighter. Whether you're called to fix a blocked toilet, get rid of some carpenter ants, or extinguish a backyard burn that got out of control, you'll head out with the tools you expect you'll need. As important as the tools is your training: you know what to do in each of these situations.

It's no different with Christians, except that we are equipped for Kingdom work. Because of our commitment to Christ, we are uniquely able to share the gospel. In addition to this general mandate to witness to the gospel message, we also bring our two categories of gifts, as John Stott explains:

> God is not a random creator; he has not given us natural gifts in order that they may be wasted. Nor is he a random redeemer, who has given us spiritual gifts to be wasted. Instead, he wants his gifts to us to be discerned, cultivated and exercised. He surely does not want us to be frustrated (because our gifts are lying idle), but rather fulfilled (because our gifts are being used).[46]

So, for example, if you've discovered after volunteering to teach Sunday School that you have a gift for teaching, consider seriously Stott's suggestion that you cultivate this gift. Or perhaps you've got a gift for working on electrical and mechanical things. Perhaps this too is a gift you should look at more closely.

You may have been uncovering other gifts in your repertoire, gifts that are pointing you to a career in science, or social services, or sales (or even areas not beginning with S). Continue trying to discern or confirm your natural gifts, so that you can cultivate them and heighten your readiness for Christian service.

At the same time, you will want to supplement these natural gifts with your spiritual ones. Take a close look at the passages in Romans 12, 1 Corinthians 12, and Ephesians 4 that list these spiritual gifts. If you've

---

[45] Quotes in Gordon Jackson, *Quotes for the Journey, Wisdom for the Way*, 175.
[46] John Stott: *The Disciple*, page no. unknown.

never done so, consider going online and taking one of the many tests designed to help you learn your spiritual gifts. You may learn, for instance, that you have the gift of administration. Or evangelism. Or leadership. Or hospitality. Or serving. Depending on how one counts them and deals with duplications in the three lists, there are about twenty gifts in all.

Your set of natural and spiritual gifts uniquely equips you for the tasks God has in store. For you, that may mean plunging into specific training or study. For others, perhaps you'll be looking only at interim just-need-to-pay-the-rent employment. If so, don't underestimate either the importance of this kind of work or the tools God has given you to do it well and honor Him as you do so.

Meanwhile, keep your tools in trim, at the ready. As the nineteenth century English minister and novelist Charles Kingsley said, "God will find thee work."

20: Experts in Goodness

I want you to be expert in goodness...
> — *Romans 16:19*, Revised English Bible

Malcolm Gladwell's 2008 book, *Outliers*, made the case that people who rose to the top of their fields did so because of the "10,000-hour rule." This was the idea that people like Bill Gates and the Beatles had put in enormous amounts of "practice" in their sphere of activity. The book soared to the top of the bestseller lists. It popularized the notion that success took long hours of commitment.

This premise drew criticism as being over-simplistic. One needed certain innate skills or a good genetic legacy to become an NBA basketball player, the critics argued; if you were physically ill-equipped, no matter how much you practiced you could never make it to the top.

Still, regardless of the validity of Gladwell's thesis, which could be paraphrased as that old adage, "Practice makes perfect," there's a powerful lesson here for Christians. Paul, writing to the Romans, urges them to become "expert in goodness." That's how the *Revised English Bible* translates it, using wording similar to that of the J. B. Phillips version. Most other translations speak of needing to become "wise in what is good" or variations on that theme.

The message is clear: Christians need to become specialists (for that's what an expert is) in goodness and wisdom. How do we get there? The same way as the punchline in that old joke about a visitor to New York asking how to get to Carnegie Hall, and the local responds, "Practice, man; practice."

So too with us. Like the beginning pianist or teacher or soccer player, or whatever sphere you choose, you need hours and hours of hard work at your craft before you can attain expert status. Paul indicates what our default behavior ought to be at all times, when he tells Titus: "Remind the people to be subject to rulers and authorities, to be obedient, to be ready to do whatever is good..." There it is again: the need *to be ready* — in this case, "to do whatever is good."

The overarching goal, as Jesus told His disciples, is that we are to "Be perfect ... as your heavenly Father is perfect." (Mt. 5:48) Virtually every translation uses the word "perfect." But the *Amplified* version gives a helpful expansion on this word: "You, therefore, must be perfect [growing into complete maturity of godliness in mind and character, having reached the proper height of virtue and integrity], as your heavenly Father is perfect." Unpacking the meaning of the Greek makes Jesus' expectation of us sound more workable an objective than just being told, "be perfect."

The Message similarly expands the implication of "be perfect": "In a word, what I'm saying is, *Grow up*. You're Kingdom subjects. Now live like it. Live out your God-created identity."

21: The Painter: A Parable[47]

The story is told of one of those genius painters during the Italian renaissance who was working on his next masterpiece. He needed a model, ideally a young boy of nine or ten, with a waif-like look. He spent hours scouring the marketplace where people gathered until he finally identified a child who would be perfect for the painting he envisaged: The child was grubby, with tousled blond hair, poorly clothed, and with a naïvely innocent expression.

The painter told the boy's mother that he wanted the boy to pose for him over a number of weeks, and that he'd pay so much up front and the rest upon completion of the sittings. The mother agreed, took the initial payment, and agreed to bring her ten-year-old son to the painter's studio on Monday at 9 a.m.

Monday came, and so did the mother and child. However, she had taken the initial payment to buy the boy new clothing, scrubbed his face till it was spotless, and perfectly groomed his hair. She wanted her son to look his best. Gone was the appearance of the waif the painter had seen, and so was the boy's earlier expression. Dressed up as he was, his face now exuded a look of pride and self-confidence that was of no use to the painter.

Disappointed, the painter explained to the woman why he could no longer use her son as a model. Her best intentions had ruined the painter's plan. He paid her a few more coins and sent her on her way.

~~~~~

As you look to the next steps on your journey, you wonder in your more earnest moments how God could use someone like you. Despite your best intentions, you stumble into sin. You struggle to control your temper. Or you have difficulty resisting gossip, both in receiving and dispensing modes. Often you seem to go along with the crowd rather than living out your convictions. Your prayer life is erratic. You are reminded of the king of England who ruled from 978 to 1016, whose incompetence earned him the title "Æthelred the Unready." You suspect God may have you listed in the Book of Life as "Marissa the Unready" or "Peter the Unready."

Not to worry. Like that ten-year-old prospective model, you are

---

[47] This entry is adapted from Gordon S. Jackson: *Your Photo on God's Fridge Door.*

wanted just as you are. God doesn't need you to put on new clothes or get your hair done. Instead, as the words of the nineteenth century hymn has it, God seeks you "Just as I am, without one plea, but that thy blood was shed for me." No need to make changes, in appearance or in your heart; just come as you are. Of course, God doesn't want us to stay as we are. As that bumper sticker says, "Please be patient: God isn't finished with me yet." But His astonishing openness to our *starting point* (no matter our condition) is what's amazing.

Note for example who gets invited in Jesus' parable of the man throwing a banquet. After the initial invitees come up with lame, even insulting, excuses why they will no longer come to this undoubtedly lavish meal, we read: "The servant came back and reported this to his master. Then the owner of the house became angry and ordered his servant, 'Go out quickly into the streets and alleys of the town and bring in the poor, the crippled, the blind and the lame.'" (Lk. 14:21) Notice that it's the poor, the crippled, the blind and the lame who are invited — the outcasts, the shabbily dressed and those utterly unable to raise their standing in life. You don't need to get into a certain tax bracket, get out of your wheelchair, or have cataract surgery so you can see properly and get around on your own.

You have been summoned. There is now neither the need nor the time to get your act together; from God's perspective, you're ready just as you are.

22: Preparation and Planning

Planning is bringing the future into the present so that you can do something about it now.

— Alan Lakein[48]

Jesus was a planner. We could say that everything about His incarnation, His ministry, His crucifixion and His resurrection were all planned by God His Father. Jesus, in carrying out His Father's plan, was always forward looking, a principle He shared with His disciples—both in instruction and by example. He taught them, for instance, to think ahead: "Suppose one of you wants to build a tower. Won't you first sit down and estimate the cost to see if you have enough money to complete it? For if you lay the foundation and are not able to finish it, everyone who sees it will ridicule you, saying, 'This person began to build and wasn't able to finish.'" (Lk. 14:28-30)

Similarly, we see an example of His planning when He prepared for the Last Supper with the twelve. Let us look at this passage in Mark:

> *On the first day of the Festival of Unleavened Bread, when it was customary to sacrifice the Passover lamb, Jesus' disciples asked him, "Where do you want us to go and make preparations for you to eat the Passover?" So he sent two of his disciples, telling them, "Go into the city, and a man carrying a jar of water will meet you. Follow him. Say to the owner of the house he enters, 'The Teacher asks: Where is my guest room, where I may eat the Passover with my disciples?' He will show you a large room upstairs, furnished and ready. Make preparations for us there." The disciples left, went into the city and found things just as Jesus had told them. So they prepared the Passover. (Mk. 14:12-16)*

Note that Jesus had anticipated this event, lining up the room and the man carrying a jar of water, which was normally a woman's duty. The man would thus have stood out among the Passover crowds milling around in the city. It is unclear how the timing worked so that the man with the jar happened on the scene exactly when the two disciples showed up; he almost certainly wasn't walking around the city all day, lugging a water jar in the hope that a couple of men would approach him for

---

[48] Alan Lakein: *How to Get Control of Your Time and Your Life*, 25.

directions. But this was the connection on which Jesus told the two disciples to rely.

Knowing how the authorities were plotting to arrest Him, Jesus prepared for this meal with noteworthy secrecy. The arrangements almost sound like something out of a spy novel, with the location of the meal unknown even to the disciples until the last minute. The disciples even have a kind of password to ask the owner of the home: "The teacher asks: Where is my guest room...?"

Then the group arrived later to prepare for the meal, "which would have involved getting the bread, wine, bitter herbs and a sauce made of dried fruit, spices and wine, and roasting the Passover lamb."[49]

What about us, when it comes to planning and preparing? The old proverb is apposite here: Man proposes, God disposes. We may take the initiative but God always has the last word. And lest there be any misunderstanding, we *should* be taking the initiative and using our common sense and good judgment to plan our next steps. We plan for a capital campaign at our church or a Christian college we're involved with. We prepare for our upcoming wedding. We plan for our youth group's mission trip to Honduras.

Unlike our secular friends, however, we plan in the context of (1) seeking to do so in keeping with God's will, and (2) knowing that He may override, modify or completely thwart our plans.

Let us conclude with two verses. The first speaks to our need to plan: "Depend on the LORD in whatever you do, and your plans will succeed." (Prov. 16:3, *New Century Version*) The second confirms yet again that we serve a God who plans. Speaking through Jeremiah to the Jewish captives in Babylon, the Lord says: "'For I know the plans I have for you,' declares the LORD, 'plans to prosper you and not to harm you, plans to give you hope and a future.'" (Jer. 29:11)

To paraphrase Lakein's definition we cited above, we could say that planning from a Christian perspective is "bringing a God-controlled future into the present so that you can implement His will today." In other words, we're getting ready today to be ready for God's tomorrow.

---

[49] *Africa Bible Commentary*, 1,195.

23: Preparing Dinner

Have you ever noticed how much time biblical characters spend preparing food? At times it's for unexpected guests. Think of the occasion when three strangers arrive at Abraham's doorstep (or tent flap, to be more accurate). He immediately offers customary Middle Eastern hospitality, with something to drink and a meal. He gets Sarah to bake some bread and orders a servant to slaughter a calf. He also brings them curds and milk. Notice two things in this episode, quite apart from their strange prediction about Sarah having a child. The first is that Abraham tells Sarah to use the finest flour, and "a choice, tender calf" is selected: no leftovers for these strangers, only the best Abraham could offer.

Of course, this meal will take a long time to prepare. It's not as if the servant could do a Costco run for a ready-to-go rotisserie chicken. There's no microwave to hasten things along. The preparation is a long, protracted business. It turns out that these three strangers are angels, God's messengers to assure Abraham and Sarah that He has not forgotten His promises. As the writer to the Hebrews points out, "Do not forget to show hospitality to strangers, for by so doing some people have shown hospitality to angels without knowing it." (Heb. 13:2) Abraham unwittingly entertains strangers who are even more important guests than he realized.

Let's look at two more examples. In the story of the prodigal son another prize calf meets its demise, as the thrilled father, like Abraham, orders only the best to mark the return of his formerly insolent but now penitent son, the one who has now returned home. The father proclaims, "Let's have a feast and celebrate. For this son of mine was dead and is alive again; he was lost and is found." (Lk. 15:23-24) No perfunctory tea and biscuits for the returning son; no, it's a full scale feast, befitting this occasion of great joy.

Finally, let's consider the feeding of the 5,000, another impromptu event. This time, though, there was no fattened calf on hand. Even though the psalmist rightly noted that God owns "the cattle on a thousand hills" (Ps. 50:10), apparently none of them were available that day to satisfy the increasingly hungry crowd described in John 6. Perplexed though the disciples were with the limited resources (five small barley loaves and two small fish), as always Jesus was prepared to handle the situation—this time with a kind of catering tour de force you don't learn in culinary school.

~~~~~

We have limited ourselves here to just three situations involving meals. We could have explored how God provided quail and manna during the Israelites' desert journey, or the meal steeped in deceit when Jacob tricked his brother Esau out of his birthright. Many others could have been included as well.

But these three situations will suffice to make one key observation about these biblical examples of preparing meals. Each involves empathy. For Abraham, it was anticipating and responding to the needs of three travelers, who would soon be hungry, if they weren't already. In the parable of the returning son, the father empathizes with astonishing magnanimity the mindset of this humiliated son. We sense the depth of the young man's shame in the words of the speech he practiced before arriving home. The father puts himself in the son's shoes and races to him in welcome. He thus deflects the ridicule or tormenting of the other villagers who would otherwise be inclined to laugh at or mock this returning failure, no doubt shabbily dressed and downcast as he anticipates his father's negative response. Yet everything the father does is exactly the opposite of what the son expected, as the father joyously celebrates the son's return. Indeed, as we have seen, his arrival triggers a full-blown feast.

Finally, with the feeding of the 5,000, Jesus displays His empathy for their increasing hunger. It is no coincidence that one of Jesus' temptations during His forty-day fast was to turn stones into bread; He knew what hunger meant. So it's no surprise that in instituting the Last Supper, He gave us food and drink—His body and His blood—to sustain us spiritually.

Both physical and spiritual food are needed to ready us for what lies ahead. You may have encountered the acronym, HALT, which warns us not to make important decisions when we are Hungry, Angry, Lonely or Tired. If we are in any of these states, so the advice goes, we are vulnerable to making ill-considered rather than thoughtful decisions. Just as we are warned after certain medical procedures not to drive and certainly not to operate heavy equipment, so too is our judgment likely to be impaired until our hunger is satisfied. Only then will our readiness for thoughtful engagement be possible. So it is no coincidence that Jesus is concerned to address our spiritual hunger. Paul's words remind us of the mysterious spiritual meal that Jesus provides for us, each time we take communion:

> *The Lord Jesus, on the night He was betrayed, took bread, and when He had given thanks, He broke it and said, "This is My body, which is for you; do this in remembrance of Me." In the same way, after supper He took the cup, saying, "This cup is the new covenant in*

My blood; do this, as often as you drink it, in remembrance of Me."
For as often as you eat this bread and drink this cup, you proclaim the
Lord's death until He comes. (1 Cor. 11:23-26)

Giving us His body and His blood is the ultimate act of empathy, as He gave His life for us, so that we are made ready for Jesus' service — thanks to this most profound and mysterious meal that feeds us spiritually time after time.

PART 4: Dealing with Unreadiness

24: Defining Unreadiness

If defining "Christian readiness" in Chapter 3 was straightforward, defining its opposite is equally so. It means, well, *not* being in a state of readiness. While that's obvious, it may be more fruitful to probe *why* this is so. What conditions might cause us to be "unready"? We can identify at least three.

But first let's imagine that you're twenty-four years old and you've been a youth pastor at a small country church for three years. You almost certainly are not ready to serve as the new senior pastor at First Global Megachurch, which has a staff of twenty-three people and four worship services on Sunday. Total Sunday attendance is in the 14,000 range.

So, are you a likely candidate for this role? Even *remotely* likely? No. Of course, we serve a God who specializes in the "only remotely" likely; think of Gideon and his unlikely victory over the Midianites. Or the unlikelihood of Abraham and Sarah having a child at her advanced age. Yes, God *could* propel you, against all odds, into this position. But almost everyone on the planet would agree you're not ready for such a role. Is that your fault? Of course not. You're also not ready to perform open heart surgery or mediate peace between the Palestinians and the Israelis. Nor are those states of unreadiness somehow your fault.

So perhaps we should refine our understanding of "unreadiness," or else our list of things we're not equipped to do would be endless. (I, for one, am not ready to fly an Airbus 380, lead a group of Navy SEALs on a commando raid, or conduct the London Philharmonic.)

Maybe our understanding of unreadiness, then, should be limited to those things for which we *could* reasonably be expected to be ready — if not now, at some time soon. I'll never be ready to fly that Airbus. But then, nobody is expecting that I might do so, either tomorrow or in ten years' time. They are entitled, however, to expect that if you are a trained ER physician, you should be ready for whatever this Friday night's mix of craziness characterizes your hospital. So that is the first of our three "conditions of unreadiness": there's a task or role that is beyond your ability. Moreover, you are on no trajectory toward being able to fill that role in the future. You, like me, have neither any plans, nor any aptitude, for flying that Airbus 380 in even the distant future.

It's another matter, though, if you have some God-given potential in a particular area, potential that needs to be cultivated before you'd be fully ready to take on a responsibility for which you're not yet equipped. This is our second type of unreadiness: You're not entirely ready at this stage but you're heading in the right direction. For an example of someone who did exactly that, see Chapter 30 concerning Dr. Margaret Brand. In this case, we expect that you'd be willing to learn and cultivate your potential; your background thus far has prepared you to engage in such learning.

Then there's our third category. We harken back to our discussion of the Five Foolish Bridesmaids, in Chapter 2. As Jesus told that story, it was plain that these bridesmaids were expected to be ready. They knew their responsibility and they knew what was expected of them. Yet they let the bridegroom down because of their carelessness.

They are the equivalent of those Christians of whom more is expected but who are lagging behind on the spiritual growth chart. Paul has some blunt words for the Christians in Corinth, when he says: "I gave you milk, not solid food, for you were not yet ready for it. Indeed, you are still not ready. You are still worldly." (2 Cor. 3:2-3)

So where does that leave us? For the most part, the "reasonableness" test we proposed a moment ago offers us a commonsense approach to discerning whether we are ready to do what we believe is God's will in a particular setting.

And yet… We need to leave room for the "unreasonableness" of our God, and His working in our lives. As novelist William Golding put it in *The Spire*:

> *Even in the old days He never asked men to do what was reasonable. Men can do that for themselves. They can buy and sell, heal and govern. But then out of some deep place comes the command to do what makes no sense at all — to build a ship on dry land; to sit among the dunghills; to marry a whore; to set their son on the altar of sacrifice. Then, if men have faith, a new thing comes.*

Golding could have written, if Christians are ready to act in faith, even when they are not ready, then "a new thing comes."

Following the father who implored Jesus to heal his demon-possessed son by saying, "I do believe; help me overcome my unbelief," (Mk. 9:24) we can restate that as "I am ready; help me to overcome my unreadiness."

25: Keeping Watch⁵⁰

I will stand at my watch and station myself on the ramparts; I will look to see what he will say to me ...

— Habakkuk 2:1

For these are the words of the Lord to me: "Go, post a watchman to report what he sees."

— Isaiah 21:6, Revised English Bible

Having defined unreadiness, we need an antidote. It is the need to keep watch. And if there's anyone who needs to be ready, it is a sentry or lookout. Whether it is a military setting, or the sailor in the crow's nest on an old sailing ship, someone who falls asleep or won't pay attention should not be assigned the task of deliberate, purposeful watching. The stakes are too high to entrust to someone who's not in a perpetual state of readiness to watch out for the wellbeing of the city, the military camp, or the ship's company.

But whether it is daytime or night, the watchmen face an odd challenge: They never know for sure what they are looking for. Almost always the sentry is noticing nothing, while looking for anything that's out of place: an unexpected movement here, an unexplained light there. In the physical world, the lookout's duty is simple: keep scanning the environment for signs of change, especially threats.

William Barclay, in his commentary on Revelation, notes how the seemingly impregnable city of Sardis was twice invaded because of complacency: the authorities didn't bother to post watchmen because they thought an attack was inconceivable. They weren't ready when the surprise attacks came.

Commenting on the letter to this church, Barclay says: "Watchfulness should be the constant attitude of the Christian life."⁵¹ He cites Paul, who writes, "Be watchful, stand firm in the faith..." (1 Cor. 16:13, *English Standard Version*), and adds that the Christian must be on guard against the wiles of Satan and false teaching.

In brief, Christians need to be alert to what's going on in the world

---

⁵⁰ This chapter is excerpted in part from Gordon S. Jackson: *Be Thou My Vision: Light, Sight and the Christian Faith.*
⁵¹ William Barclay, *The Daily Study Bible: Revelation, vol. 1*, 118.

around them, watching for possible threats and opportunities. Is there a threat to mission work in a particular country because of rising anti-Christian hostility, that might lead individual Christians either to adopt a lower profile than usual, or perhaps even leave the country? Or are there perhaps outreach opportunities in your neighborhood to reach single moms that your church should pursue? Crucial to the Christian's "watchman role" is attentiveness and bringing what is seen on the horizon to the attention of others.

In Scripture, the watchman had to be ready for three tasks: Watch for signs of danger, especially military threat; be alert for messengers bringing news; and note changes in the society. It may be that, like King David and his followers, they are awaiting news on the outcome of a battle — and are scouring the horizon for a messenger who will bring word, of victory or defeat.[52]

Christians also have a watchman role that is internally focused, on their need for attentiveness and vigilance. As Peter notes, "Be on the alert! Wake up! Your enemy the devil, like a roaring lion, looking for someone to devour." (1 Pet. 5:8, *Revised English Bible*) While Peter's remarks may apply equally to the church generally, they certainly speak to the individual Christian's need to stay alert. As the notes on this verse in the *NIV Study Bible* point out, "Perhaps Peter remembered his own difficulty in keeping awake during our Lord's agony in Gethsemane." (See Mt. 26:36-46)

This emphasis on the need for Jesus' followers to be alert is rooted in His own teaching to the disciples, as we saw in the parable of the bridesmaids. As the *NIV* puts it, instead of staying alert like the five wise virgins, the five foolish ones "became drowsy and fell asleep." After concluding the parable with the somber word that this group was shut out from the wedding banquet, Jesus says, "Therefore keep watch, because you do not know the day or the hour." (Mt. 25:13)

Elsewhere, Jesus gives the same warning to His disciples in connection with the end times, vividly pictured in *The Message*: "But be on your guard. Don't let the sharp edge of your expectation get dulled by parties and drinking and shopping. Otherwise, that Day is going to take you by complete surprise, spring on you suddenly like a trap, for it's going to come on everyone, everywhere, at once. So, whatever you do, don't go to sleep at the switch." (Lk. 21:34-35, *The Message*)

Just as Habukkuk watched for possible enemy attack in a physical

---

[52] For example, we read in 2 Samuel 18:24 that "While David was sitting between the inner and outer gates, the watchman went up to the roof of the gateway by the wall." The watchman saw one runner, then another, bringing word of the battle involving David's rebellious son Absalom — and that he had been killed.

setting, so too should Christians be conscious of their weak spots and "posting sentries" to guard against the temptations they find most common or strongest.[53] As we grow in our individual faith, our watchfulness should help us identify the kinds of temptations that keep coming back—and thus heighten our readiness as Jesus' disciples to address both threats and opportunities.

The set of sentries you will need to post will differ from mine. But all Christians have in common the need to rely on a "watchman mindset." This entails being aware of our vulnerabilities. Jesus not only taught us in the Lord's prayer to say, "Lead us not into temptation," (Lk. 11:4) He also promises the presence of the Holy Spirit in our lives.[54] It is the Holy Spirit, of course, who will play the "sentry" role if we allow Him to.

The sentry's main task is to ask, "Who goes there?" and to block entry to undesirables. As Thomas À Kempis puts it, "[W]hen temptation first appears, we must be especially alert, because it is easier to defeat the enemy if we do not allow him to set foot inside the door of the mind but meet him on the step as he knocks."[55]

Unlike the sentry, the watchman's contribution, in the church and in our individual lives, is to serve as an early warning system. If he sees a possible attack coming from the north, he will alert the officers who will in turn strengthen the guard on that flank, posting as many troops, or sentries, as possible. For the most part, though, the watchman is not a person of action; his role is preeminently concerned with watching. In doing this, he is in some ways simply mirroring what God Himself does for His people. The psalmist assures us that "He who watches over you will not slumber; indeed, he who watches over Israel will neither slumber nor sleep." (Ps. 121:3-4)

Like the disciples in Gethsemane, sleeping followers are of little use to Jesus when He calls us to be awake. Rather, we are to aspire to be the kind of watchman Isaiah describes: "All day long I stand on the watchtower, Lord, and night after night I am at my post." (Is. 21:8, *Revised English Bible*) God asked nothing more of this watchman, and He asks nothing less of us.

---

[53] See Chapter 18 for a more detailed treatment of this concept.
[54] Jn. 15:26, Jn. 16:7 and elsewhere.
[55] Thomas À Kempis, *The Imitation of Christ*. Translated by Betty Knott, 54.

26: Crossing the Jordan

After the death of Moses the servant of the LORD, the LORD said to Joshua son of Nun, Moses' aide: "Moses my servant is dead. Now then, you and all these people, get ready to cross the Jordan River into the land I am about to give to them...."

— *Joshua 1:1-2*

Tomorrow you start your new job. Or it's your first day at college. Or perhaps it's your wedding day. Whatever the occasion, you are now poised to cross a Jordan River of your own—a major, life-changing step, one that will parallel those of the priests who at Joshua's command stepped into the river to lead the Israelites across. Notice though the conditions under which they did so: "Now the Jordan is at flood stage all during harvest." We're talking here about a river that's in flood, not a gently meandering stream. "Yet as soon as the priests who carried the ark reached the Jordan and their feet touched the water's edge, the water from upstream stopped flowing." (Josh. 3:15-16) Now we're talking about the faith of priests who trusted that God knew what He was doing in requiring them to take that crucial first step. (Without, please note, life jackets or the presence of lifeguards.) Yet their high-risk behavior is exactly what God required of those men in that moment.

You are as ready as you can be for this next chapter in your life. You've presumably done whatever preparation you can. And while you may be anxious about what lies ahead, you know that you can hand your uncertainties over to God. Like the children of Israel entering the Promised Land, you know that God's hand has been over your journey thus far, and it will continue to be on you as you move ahead. A difference, though, is that your "crossing the Jordan" experience is unlikely to be accompanied by a dramatically visible miracle comparable to what these priests, and the nation they represented, encountered that day. Don't for a moment doubt that the God who is bringing you to the brink of your own Jordan experience knows exactly how to get you across. As Lynne Bundesen puts it, "[God] has not forgotten how to part the sea."[56] Or your Jordan.

---

[56] Lynn Bundesen: *One Prayer at a Time*. No page number.

27: Send Me!

Then I heard the voice of the Lord saying, "Whom shall I send? And who will go for us?"
And I said, "Here am I. Send me!"

— *Isaiah 6:8*

In this awe-inspiring account of Isaiah's call we encounter something different in the way God intrudes on His servants' lives. With Moses and Gideon, for example, in the Old Testament, or with Jesus calling His disciples, the pattern is that these men are recruited to a particular task. Moses is to lead the Israelites out of Egypt; Gideon to free them from the Midianites; and the disciples to become Jesus' apprentices (although at this early stage they can have little idea what that will entail).

Isaiah's experience is different. First comes a general call: "Whom shall I send?" Where? To do what? When? Isaiah knows no details whatever. This call doesn't come with a job description; there's no fine print for him to read before signing up. Yet here's the striking thing: he accepts the call anyway. He's like someone volunteering for the military, who undertakes to go on any mission, whatever the commanding officer decrees.

What brings Isaiah to the point where he can so unhesitatingly sign a contract whose details God will fill in later? One thing is the vision he has experienced of God's holiness. Read verses 1-4 in this chapter to get a sense of what he saw. The vision leads him to realize his utter unworthiness to be in God's presence, let alone feel qualified to serve him. God's holiness has shown up his sinfulness.

The second factor is the solution to that problem: "Then one of the seraphim flew to me with a live coal in his hand, which he had taken with tongs from the altar. With it he touched my mouth and said, 'See, this has touched your lips; your guilt is taken away and your sin atoned for.'" (Is. 6:6-7) Thus cleansed, Isaiah is now freed, equipped and ready for kingly service, whatever the task.

Centuries later, John the Baptist "...saw Jesus coming toward him and said, 'Look, the Lamb of God, who takes away the sin of the world!'" (Jn. 1:29) Now, it's not only one man being cleansed and equipped for an as-yet unspecified ministry, it's *all* of us who see Jesus as our Lord. And like Isaiah, we too are now able to say, "Here am I. Send me."

28: Four Out of Five Ain't Bad

Imagine you're on the way to the airport for a vacation abroad. You do a last-minute mental inventory.[57]

1. Travel insurance? Check.
2. Boarding pass and ticket info? Check.
3. Credit cards? Check.
4. Luggage, including your meds? Check.
5. Passport?

Passport? Oops. You now realize that it's in your safety deposit box at your bank. You're unlikely to keep going and say, "Well, four out of five isn't bad. It'll be okay."

Well, would you say you are "mostly ready" for your trip? The fact is, however, that not having your passport is a deal breaker. The airline staff won't let you board without one. In this case, "mostly ready" isn't good enough.

What of other instances where "mostly ready" is acceptable? Imagine you're a fifth-grade teacher who is new to this state. You've been hired to teach but your certification is provisional; you still need to take three credit hours of instruction on the history of your new state. So, for all practical purposes, you're ready to teach these fifth graders. But from the perspective of the state's education board, you're not yet truly and completely and fully ready.

How to apply the concept of "mostly ready" to our faith? Perhaps the best answer comes from asking this question: Are you as ready as God can reasonably expect you to be? The teacher who is new to the state is otherwise as ready as she can be; it's no fault of hers that there's another hoop through which she has to jump. But the "mostly ready" scenario regarding the passport is in a different league. You goofed. You weren't as ready as you should have been.

One's degree of readiness in these scenarios is easy to determine. That's not the case with spiritual readiness, which by definition is more abstract and resistant to precise measures. Still, as we saw in Chapter 6, on how to attain readiness, our focus ought always to be on enhancing our

---

[57] This chapter is based on an entry in Gordon S. Jackson: *Your Photo on God's Fridge Door.*

relationship with our Lord. If our spiritual journey is currently characterized by a limp, we need God's therapy to walk or perhaps even run unimpeded.

29: Self-Imposed Unreadiness

[E]ven the darkness will not be dark to you; the night will shine like the day,
for darkness is as light to you.

— Psalm 139:12

The concept of learned helplessness came into psychology in the middle of the last century.[58] At the risk of oversimplifying it, the idea is that if people repeatedly experience a negative and stressful situation that is beyond their control, they may reach the point where they give up trying to deal with it. That applies even if circumstances change to make it easier to meet the challenge.

The Medical News Today website says, "Once a person having this experience discovers that they cannot control events around them, they lose motivation. Even if an opportunity arises that allows the person to alter their circumstances, they do not take action."[59] The site gives as an example someone who has tried repeatedly to stop smoking but failed; he or she eventually concludes that it will never happen and is resigned to accepting it will never happen. Or think of a schoolchild volunteering the answer to a question and told by the teacher that her answer is wrong. Same with the child's next answer. And the third. Soon enough, the child is going to stop volunteering, convinced that she is a poor student. If this occurred over an extended period, the child may well withdraw into herself and define herself as a failure—and not offer any answers at all.

The experience of repeated inability to deal with a stressful situation, like child or spouse abuse, therefore leads to an assumption of futility that may be associated with depression. An abused child, for example, whose self-esteem has been shattered may struggle to respond well to a loving situation if he is removed from his traumatic environment. Both children and adults may need extended counseling to help them overcome their learned helplessness.

For Christians, the result is that they no longer care about being in a

---

[58] This chapter is based on a section of Gordon S. Jackson: *Your Photo on God's Fridge Door*.

[59]
https://www.medicalnewstoday.com/articles/325355#:~:text=In%20psycholog
y%2C%20learned%20helplessness%20is,opportunities%20for%20change%20beco
me%20available. Accessed Sept. 4, 2023.

state of readiness. They may be on the verge of despair. Whatever spiritual passion they may have enjoyed seems to have evaporated. What can Christians learn from this notion of learned helplessness?

We can at times find a parallel in our spiritual lives. It's termed "the dark night of the soul." The term was originated by St. John of the Cross, a sixteenth-century Spanish mystic. It refers to a bleak, desolate stretch in one's spiritual life when God seems remote or even totally absent. Many prominent Christians have suffered from this ordeal, sometimes for long periods. For instance, a 2007 *Time* magazine article on Mother Teresa noted that she experienced grave doubts and spiritual darkness from 1948 onwards, more or less continuously until shortly before her death in 1997. So did Martin Luther and countless other Christians through the ages.

Their experience may not have been a *learned* helplessness, but they led to a sense of helplessness nonetheless. For by its very nature nothing seems to "work" as one tries to extricate oneself from this grim condition, something like the equivalent of depression in the spiritual realm. Prayer doesn't accomplish anything. Nor does Bible study or counseling. Nor can one "just snap out of it," as Mother Teresa and Martin Luther would tell us if they were still with us.

One feels far from ready to do anything in God's Kingdom. We may pray as earnestly as ever, yet it seems that God neither hears nor responds. As E. M. Blaiklock says, "It is one of the sternest tests of faith when God appears not to care, to be inactive, dead."[60] During these dark days it may be tempting to give up on one's faith. No doubt many have. But just as victims of learned helplessness can surmount the experiences that have dragged them down, there is hope for Christians struggling with the dark night of the soul. As Edmond Rostand said, "It is at night that faith in light is admirable."[61] A difference though is that our "daybreak" lies in God's hands, not those of therapists. Until then, we can only cling to a God Whom we assert by blind faith is good, loving, and despite the surrounding darkness, has neither forgotten nor abandoned us. Mystified though we may be at this moment at God's seeming absence, we need to reflect on what we knew before the darkness fell and heed the words of V. Raymond Edman: "Never doubt in the dark what God told you in the light."[62]

Meanwhile, if you are grappling with this kind of spiritual darkness, be alert for those glimmers of light that God may send your way. Beware of becoming so resigned to your darkness that you no longer expect God's light again, like someone with learned helplessness, and refuse to

---

[60] E. M. Blaiklock: *Commentary on the Psalms*, vol. 1, 44.
[61] Quoted in Gordon S. Jackson: *Quotes for the Journey, Wisdom for the Way*, 54.
[62] Quoted in Gordon S. Jackson: *Quotes for the Journey, Wisdom for the Way*. 44.

recognize "a way out" when it appears. Recall that no matter how despondent you may feel, you serve a God Who scoffs at the word "helpless." And recall too that you serve a God who can help restore you fully to a state of readiness for His purposes in His Kingdom.

30: You'll Know When You Get There

Joshua is deservedly one of the Bible's great heroes. Taking the mantle of leadership from Moses was the most daunting of tasks. Joshua Chapter 1 sees God repeatedly urging the new leader to have courage, courage grounded in the reality that God Himself would be with him.[63]

His first major assignment is to lead the children of Israel into the Promised Land as they miraculously cross the Jordan. The circumstances of the crossing must have boosted yet again Joshua's sense of God's presence and power.

But then came Jericho, a powerful, well-fortified city that stood as an apparently insurmountable roadblock to the conquest of the Promised Land. There was no way the Israelites could possess the Promised Land without dealing with this fortress city. What is Joshua to do? What miracle will God do next to deal with Jericho? What will Joshua's part be in this next step of Canaan's conquest? Curiously, though, before we get the odd set of instructions about marching around the city and blowing trumpets, we have this encounter between Joshua and an angel:

> *Now when Joshua was near Jericho, he looked up and saw a man standing in front of him with a drawn sword in his hand. Joshua went up to him and asked, "Are you for us or for our enemies?"*
>
> *"Neither," he replied, "but as commander of the army of the Lord I have now come." Then Joshua fell facedown to the ground in reverence, and asked him, "What message does my Lord have for His servant?" The commander of the Lord's army replied, "Take off your sandals, for the place where you are standing is holy." And Joshua did so. (Josh. 3:13-15)*

What's noteworthy in this encounter is that there's nothing about how Joshua should attack Jericho. That comes later. First, it appears that Joshua needs to be reminded that he's proceeding from holy ground as he's planning his attack on Jericho. With due reverence he asks the angel for a message. Instead of a detailed battle plan, which he receives only later and directly from God, the angel tells him to take off his shoes. That's lesson number one. When we're facing a huge challenge or seemingly insurmountable problem, remember we are to move ahead only after

---

[63] See Chapter 18 on Joshua's master grace.

grounding ourselves with the knowledge that God is to accompany us.

Lesson number two is that we'll get our instructions in good time – that is, in *God's* good time, which may mean later than we'd like. Matthew Henry provides a useful illustration in this regard: "Admirals, sometimes, when they are sent abroad, are not to open their commission till they have got so many leagues off at sea...."[64] We see a modern day parallel in two 1960s movies, "Dr. Strangelove" and "Fail Safe." The first is a dark satire, the second a tense thriller. Both deal with the theme of nuclear bombers incorrectly sent to attack the Soviet Union. In each, we see the pilots and crew open their instructions about their targets only after they believe they're committed to an attack.

For the rest of us, though, like Joshua we'll know what to do as we approach our own point of need. We can be confident that, with God's help, we'll be ready when the moment arrives. Meanwhile, let's be sure to remain standing on holy ground.

---

[64] Matthew Henry: *One-Volume Commentary on the Bible*, 1,145.

31: Learning on the Job

Unlike Joshua, who was initially given no clear instruction on how to conquer Jericho, we may receive an unmistakable God-given assignment — but one that we know is far beyond our current competence.

Which brings us to Paul and Margaret Brand. Dr. Paul Brand was a legendary missionary doctor, known for his pioneering work in India, treating leprosy. He recounts his love affair with medicine and the marvel of the human body in his book, *Fearfully and Wonderfully Made*, co-authored with Philip Yancey.

Less well known is *Vision for God*, written by Margaret Brand, Paul's wife. She too was a medical doctor, working alongside Paul in India. One day she got a call from a colleague at a missionary-run eye clinic, asking Margaret to join her in treating the patients suffering from a wide range of vision problems. Margaret protested that she had no specialist training in ophthalmology. She was stating the truth, in all humility, that she wasn't prepared. But her colleague wouldn't have any excuses and insisted she join her. "You'll learn," she said. "Please start on Monday."[65]

She did both. She began that next Monday. And she began to learn, especially about the impact of leprosy on her patients' eyes. Although her book is quite different from her husband's better-known publication, it too is well worth reading to learn of the impact she had in a medical specialty for which she was initially quite unprepared.

Matthew Henry's observation three centuries before Margaret Brand anticipated her situation: "When the Spirit of the Lord comes upon [people] it will make them expert even without experience."[66] First came her commitment, without experience, but her readiness to learn subsequently equipped her to do good work (if not quite "expert") from the outset — with her expertise expanding as she kept learning.

As God did with Margaret, so too might He put us in places or situations for which we feel ill-prepared. It may be a difficult situation at work where you're called to intervene. Or you may be called upon to mediate a bitter and seemingly insoluble family fight.

You can be confident that although you lack the skills you wish were in your repertoire, if it's God who is positioning you for this new role, be

---

[65] Margaret Brand: *Vision for God*, page no. unknown.
[66] Matthew Henry: *One-Volume Commentary on the Bible*, 297.

ready to hear His word of assurance, *You'll learn,* and His expectation: *Please start on Monday.*

32: Preparing for Change

You may be happily settled in your Christian walk. In all aspects of your life, you feel that God is smiling on you. All is well: at work, at home, with friends, in your spiritual walk.

However, you know that life isn't static; inevitably you will encounter change in the days ahead. That makes you uncomfortable, as you feel prepared to handle what life is presenting you right now. You're unsure how changed circumstances might threaten your equilibrium. That's because, if you're honest, you may be uncomfortable about change. If so, prepare for what could be a rough ride.

For change is an integral part of life. You can partially prepare for its arrival by knowing what kind of changes you may encounter. The changes we face can be divided into three broad categories: the fully expected, the complete surprises, and those that come upon us more slowly.

Several biblical examples illustrate the first two types. Joshua chapter 1 describes the long-awaited changes that Moses' successor faced. Getting to the edge of the Promised Land was no surprise; this is, after all, what the children of Israel had been working, and walking, towards for forty years. Yet there's no doubt that pulses quickened as the Israelites stood next to the Jordan, contemplating the next steps that the Lord had in store for them.

Likewise, Jesus was focused throughout His ministry on heading toward the cross. He alone was not surprised by the events that led in quick succession to acclamation in Jerusalem, agony and betrayal in Gethsemane, and then the horrific events culminating in Golgotha. Yet He too had to entrust the change that He faced—an agonizing, atoning death—to God the Father, to Whom He prayed, "Into your hands I commit my spirit." (Lk. 23:46) In both these instances, the change was predictable and anticipated.

Scripture is replete with instances of the second kind of change, those developments that enter the lives of God's people totally without warning. One example comes at the beginning of Matthew's gospel: "[A]n angel of the Lord appeared to Joseph in a dream. 'Get up,' he said, 'take the child and his mother and escape to Egypt and stay there until I tell you, for Herod is going to search for the child to kill him." (Mt. 2:13) Like Gideon, Joseph is quietly getting on with life when God abruptly breaks in with unmistakable authority, telling him to take a bold step that will help accomplish God's purposes.

We can draw several lessons concerning our need for readiness from these first two kinds of changes. One is that for the predictable changes, we can be preparing for them in prayer. Do we think that Joshua only began thinking and praying about entering the Promised Land when he reached its borders? Or that Jesus first prayed about being prepared for the cross only that night in Gethsemane? Likewise, with us, we can prepare and pray for guidance long in advance of events we can expect to come our way. Even though we may be thin on specifics, as high school students we can pray generally about our choice of college or the best step to take after graduation. Or if we are in college, we can pray about the steps we will take after getting our degrees. Other changes too may be heading our way, some unwelcome but inevitable, others that we eagerly anticipate. We will be better able to handle all of them by committing them to God, even far in advance, and asking for His wisdom so we may choose well when the time comes.

What of those dramatic moments of unexpected change? Again, the change could be welcome (an unexpected promotion) or unwelcome (the sudden death of a loved one). Either way, we may be called upon at a moment's notice to seek God's help in making major decisions in response to changed circumstances.

A third category are those slower, more incremental changes that arise out of everyday life. These are the most difficult to prepare for. We slowly find ourselves becoming restless with our church, feeling we're getting less and less of the nurturing we need. Is it time to consider leaving? What are the implications for us, for our families, of such a change? Or should we stay, and what are the implications of that? These kinds of change aren't necessarily marked by a particular point in time, like a graduation date, or the sudden shock of a phone call bearing bad news. They parallel the distinction that journalists make between hard news (or events) and trends. Particular events happen at a specific time: today's basketball game, tomorrow's city council meeting. Whether the news was anticipated or not, events are easy to cover. Trends, by contrast, are much more slippery and harder to detect and write about.

Likewise with us. Because there may be no one point at which we might say it's time to seek another church, we struggle to know for sure if a decision is called for. Perhaps it's with these slow, incremental changes in our lives that we most need clarity on God's will. For God may be wanting us to change in areas where we don't yet realize change is called for. Our quest for guidance should thus be as concerned for God to help us know where we should be sensitive to possible changes that we should be making.

Then there are the times when we ought not to change. Gordon T.

Smith, in his book *Listening to God in Times of Choice*, says that unless we have clear evidence that we should leave a given situation, we should stay. "The bias should be against change."[67]

Rather than leaving the church where we feel unhappy, it may be that we should stick it out and make whatever contribution we can. By no means does God expect us to see every unpleasantness or obstacle in life as a reason to change our circumstances. The difficulty is in knowing which unpleasant circumstances call for change, and which call for endurance. That difficulty itself calls for another kind of discernment.

Change often brings discomfort or even pain. Charles Swindoll puts it this way: "God-sized assignments not only require trust, they also require major adjustments. I have never seen an exception to this rule: Major adjustments accompany God's will."[68] Even the most positive changes in our lives require adjustments and giving up something from our past. Hence, a warning: We need to prepare ourselves not only for the answers that God will give us, we need also to be ready for the accompanying discomfort that will come from responding to these changes. This isn't pleasant news if you're someone who particularly dislikes change and is deeply comforted by the known and the familiar.

Yet for our own spiritual growth, God requires that we keep growing and changing. The gospels and epistles call us to a life of discipleship and ongoing spiritual growth; the New Testament repeatedly emphasizes that God doesn't call us to be static Christians. Whether we are dealing with normal spiritual growth or transitions brought on by life's circumstances, the sooner we recognize that change is a permanent feature of our Christian walk, the better.

---

[67] Gordon T. Smith: *Listening to God in Times of Choice*, 111.
[68] Charles Swindoll: Source unknown.

PART 5: Other Readiness Issues

33: The God Who Prepares

We Christians serve a God who models those characteristics of readiness He expects in His followers. We saw in Chapter 4, for example, how Jesus displayed several qualities that prepared Him for His ministry, qualities that we would do well to emulate.

In one setting after another, Scripture points to a "preparing God." He is quite unlike the God of deists, who believe God created everything but then took off for an extended lunch and left us human beings to figure things out for ourselves. On the contrary, Christians believe that God is active, engaged, and shaping history at the macro and micro levels; He is as concerned about the war in Ukraine as He is about your next-door neighbor's battle with congestive heart failure.

Let's begin with heaven. Jesus said, "My Father's house has many rooms; if that were not so, would I have told you that I am going there to prepare a place for you?" (Jn. 14:2) His promise that He will prepare the way for us is mirrored in this comment by an unknown writer: "Heaven is a prepared place for a prepared people, and they that enter shall find that they are neither unknown nor unexpected."

Moreover, heaven's seating arrangements have been taken care of — at least, those places of honor next to Jesus. James and John let their unseemly ambition show through with their request to sit on each side of Jesus when He came into His glory. Jesus replied, "… to sit at my right or left is not for me to grant. These places belong to those for whom they have been prepared." (Mk. 10:40)

Yet another example of what has been preordained comes in the parable of the sheep and goats, in which Jesus says: "Then the King will say to those on his right, 'Come, you who are blessed by my Father; take your inheritance, the kingdom prepared for you since the creation of the world.'" (Mt: 25:34) In similar vein, Paul tells the Corinthians: "What no eye has seen, what no ear has heard, and what no human mind has conceived — the things God has prepared for those who love him." (1 Cor. 2:9)

Meanwhile, though, there's work for us to do. Here too we are anticipated. As Ephesians 2:10 puts it, "[W]e are God's handiwork, created in Christ Jesus to do good works, which God prepared in advance for us to do."

Clearly, Scripture is talking about a "preparing God," whose preparations for His people—both in this life and the next—show that contrary to what the deists may say, He's no divine being out to lunch or who took the weekend off.

34: The Martha Syndrome

They presumed to do more than it was God's will for them to do, and so they soon lost the gift of grace.

— Thomas à Kempis[69]

The Christian satirical magazine, *The Wittenburg Door*,[70] ran an article about a youth worker and his wife. Written from her point of view, she described how incredibly committed he was to serving the youth in his church: attending one event after another, supporting the kids at their school events, always available as a listening ear. "If he isn't with kids, he's thinking about them and preparing for his next encounter with them," she wrote. He was, she said, completely devoted to his ministry.

Then came her punch line. "When it comes to youth work, my husband has always been one hundred percent. I guess that's why I left him. There isn't much left after one hundred percent."

~~~~~

This misguided youth pastor became an extreme example of the Martha Syndrome. We referred to Martha briefly in Chapter 5, where we noted how irritated she was that her sister wasn't helping with all the preparations she thought were needed for Jesus' visit. Martha certainly meant well and was eager to serve Him. But there was a problem, which Thomas Green points out in his book *Darkness in the Marketplace*. Martha has until now been "working for God" — her busyness is all done out of love for Jesus. It is a gift that suited her temperament. But now Jesus tells her that this isn't the gift He really wants from her. This is a real moment of grace in her life, Green says: "If she lives through it and is able to come to peace and get beneath the surface of her hurt feelings, she may become one of those rare souls who no longer merely work for God. She may begin instead to 'do God's work.'"[71]

In other words, Green says Martha needs to distinguish between being ready to serve Jesus in the way *she* thinks He'll approve, rather than going the extra step of finding what *He* truly wants of her. Green then

---

[69] Thomas à Kempis: *The Imitation of Christ*, translation by Betty I, Knott, 122.
[70] The spelling is correct; the founders of the magazine incorrectly spelling the name of the city where Martin Luther posted his 95 Theses, Wittenberg, and decided to stick with the wrong spelling.
[71] Thomas Green: *Darkness in the Marketplace*, 48.

gives a personal example. Imagine his birthday is coming up and you'd like to give him a gift. You consider various options, but unless you know him well you're unlikely to know that he greatly enjoys blue cheese. So, if you wanted to delight him on his birthday, that's what you'd give him as a gift. Then imagine Martha were giving a gift to Jesus, with the result, Green says, that "[W]hile she finds it queer and somewhat repugnant that God should be a lover of blue cheese, she is also becoming aware that her love for him is stronger than her distaste for blue cheese."

Martha's zeal for serving Jesus, Green points out, is misplaced. She's asking the wrong question. Isn't she doing the right thing by following Jesus' example of selfless ministry? No. Instead, now is the time she should take advantage of Jesus' presence, to sit at His feet and learn what He has to share—just as her sister is doing. He knows that He will not be with them much longer and that, like Mary, Martha should focus on Him and His presence. But Martha's focus is on preparing the house, the meal, the refreshments with an increasingly grim determination as her sister refrains from helping her. We can reasonably ask if she's confusing "readiness" with a streak of martyrdom.

As always, Jesus cuts to the heart of things when He chastises her: "'Martha, Martha,' the Lord answered, 'you are worried and upset about many things, but few things are needed—or indeed only one. Mary has chosen what is better, and it will not be taken away from her.'" (Lk. 10:41-42)

Martha's misplaced readiness leads to two insights. The first is from the management consultant, Peter Drucker, who said: "There is nothing so useless as doing efficiently that which should not be done at all."[72] Then, more explicitly related to our walk with Jesus, there is the warning by Thomas à Kempis noted above, who wrote in *The Imitation of Christ* about certain over-eager saints of his day: "They presumed to do more than it was God's will for them to do, and so they soon lost the gift of grace."[73]

In short, God expects us to be ready—but not to "out-ready" ourselves. Instead of working like a Martha, doing what we think God expects our readiness to look like, perhaps we ought to be paying more attention to God's presence and expectations. Even if His preferences run to a divine equivalent of blue cheese.

---

[72] https://www.brainyquote.com/quotes/peter_drucker_105338. Accessed April 18, 2024.
[73] Thomas À Kempis, *The Imitation of Christ*. Translated by Betty Knott, 122.

35: Ready, Set, Go!

The four chapters telling the story of Jonah hold innumerable lessons for us, one of which we could title "Ready, Set, Go." Or, more accurately, "Ready, Set, Nope."

In Chapter 16 we read of the need for obedience, the need to "wake up" and get to work with what is before us. The emphasis there is *that* we should be about Kingdom work. The emphasis here is different: that we, like Jonah, are tempted to define *where* we should go. We must heed both emphases and calls to action if we are to run well the race before us, as we hear a voice saying, "Ready, set, go!"

The basic structure of Jonah's story is well known, even to those not familiar with the Bible. God calls Jonah to go and preach repentance to the Ninevites, a people notorious for their cruelty. Despite his reaction to the Lord's command, there's no disputing the fact that Jonah is *ready*. He is a prophet, after all. And God doesn't assign tasks to His servants unless they are ready. Or, if there's any question about their readiness, He fills in whatever gaps remain for His servants who set out in obedience and trust, as we saw in Chapter 24, on defining "unreadiness."

Jonah knows what's required of him: He is to tell these people about Yahweh, the only true God, and that they must repent if they are to be spared His wrath. He is equipped with a message and has the backing of the Lord Himself. He is *set* to go. Except that he doesn't. Instead of obeying the Lord, he heads to the port of Joppa, where he finds a ship bound for Tarshish. It is going in exactly the opposite direction. His plan, which in retrospect he will realize is hopelessly deluded, is "to flee from the Lord." (Jon. 1:3) How small a view he must have had of the Lord and His reach! If disobeying God were not such a serious business, Jonah's thinking would be comical. So, ready and set though he is, Jonah chooses not to *go*. Or, more accurately, he opts to go, just not where God is sending him.

We know the rest of the story. Eventually, after he rubs shoulders with death in the depths of the Mediterranean, the big fish spews him up onto dry land. Finally, he chooses to obey and goes to Nineveh. But what a resentful harbinger of God's grace and forgiveness he turns out to be. Miraculously, the Ninevites, from the humblest to the king himself, repent. But is Jonah humbled and grateful that God has used him to bring this about? You know the answer. He ends up sulking under a plant.

Like Jonah, we may be ready and set to go, so long as it's in a direction we would like. Moreover, we would like our God-given assignment to be noteworthy, certainly something befitting our important role in His Kingdom. As Dominic Smart put it,

> *We sometimes wish the Spirit would give us something spectacular to do. Mundane obedience seems pedestrian and unspiritual. But the Spirit simply says to Peter, 'Simon, three men are looking for you, so get up and go downstairs.' Remember how, when Naaman was told to go and dip in the Jordan, he protested that this was too simple, and besides, the Jordan was a filthy river. If he'd been given some spectacular and heroic challenge, he would have risen to it.*[74]

~~~~~

Unlike Jonah, our unspoken grumble may be that we've been given a task that's too modest, too insignificant. Surely God could have given us something more spectacular and heroic, a challenge to which we, like Namaan, would readily have risen.

Or perhaps not. Our heavenly Father (1) knows what He wants done infinitely better than we do, and (2) knows our egos and vanity and the barriers that they could be to serving Him. He will assign "Nineveh-level" work to the prophets who are ready for that role, whether they're willing to go there or not. Meanwhile, ninety-nine percent of the time the rest of us know what God wants us to be doing. We know both *what* He wants us to be doing, and *where* we are to do it. Logic tells us we can't be doing the "what" if we avoid the "where." As we ready ourselves for departure, we need to check our boarding pass and make sure we have the right destination: Nineveh. Not Tarshish.

---

[74] Dominic Smart: *Kingdom Builders: Witnessing, Dying, Moving*, 50-51.

36: Staged Readiness

It's a Sunday afternoon. You and your family have just returned from a week camping at your favorite lake. You are grubby, in urgent need of a shower. You also have a week's worth of stubble that's giving you an oddly dignified appearance that your two children keep teasing you about. They find your seemingly new dignity an odd contrast with your favorite T-shirt that's been with you for twenty-seven years, a garment whose tattiness is matched only by your sweatpants—about which nothing more should be said.

You get grubbier still as you clean out the camper and are still packing your equipment in the garage when your wife calls out that dinner is ready. She's now got the Chinese takeaway you picked up on the way home divided up for the four of you. (Of course, she went into the restaurant; you are such a mess that she didn't want to risk the embarrassment of anyone seeing you.)

Yes, dinner. The shower can wait...

~~~~~

The next morning you're in your three-piece suit. (Your T-shirt and sweatpants are in the laundry basket.) Your tie is immaculately knotted. Your shoes could be new, such is their shininess. The scruffiness that was aspiring to be a beard is gone. And yes, you've showered...

You've done all you could to enhance your appearance for this second-round job interview, for vice president for logistics. In short, if you were a house for sale, people would say you've been optimally staged.[75] And you have: you have optimized everything about your appearance to heighten the prospects of "selling yourself" to the company president on your suitability for this senior position. You're putting your best foot forward, as they say. You're as ready as you can be for this interview.

That's just like Joseph, when he was summoned to appear before a perplexed Pharaoh who couldn't figure out the meaning of his dreams. We read in Genesis 41:14 how he changed his clothes and shaved before

---

[75] House staging is a relatively new concept, which people embrace to varying degrees when seeking to sell their home. Some people limit themselves to moving their clutter and vacuuming; other hire a professional stager who will bring in furniture for the occasion and more or less gut your house of your stuff which is assumed to be hideously out of date and at risk of offending prospective buyers.

entering the ruler's presence. Even as a prisoner, he sought to put his best foot forward. As an unshaved, grubbily clothed prisoner he was not ready to go before Pharaoh.

Which brings us to two related aspects of readiness we have not yet considered in this book: context and authenticity. Just as you were ready when your wife announced that dinner was on the table, so too were you ready the next morning for that interview. There was nothing inappropriate about your shabby attire at the family dinner table, given that you'd all just returned from a week outdoors. But showing up in that condition the following morning would not have been well received.

"Readiness," then, is clearly contextual. We saw that too with Joseph. Neither you nor he were being deceptive; you each dressed for the occasion. Given the context, each of you behaved and conducted yourself appropriately. In the context of your job interview, your prospective boss expected you to dress appropriately – just as Joseph did in what neither he nor Pharaoh knew at the outset would also be *his* job interview, for prime minister.

A problem arises, though, when we encounter what we could call "pretend readiness" or "faked readiness." That's when we somehow fake the impression we seek to give, that we are more ready than we truly are. For example, what if you had puffed your resume, implying to your prospective boss that you were more ready for the VP role than you truly were? Or what if you were on a dating site and you stretched the truth in your online profile? ("Hey, everyone does it and everyone expects it.") How ready are you for an authentic relationship when you will lie to somebody before even meeting them in person?

Speaking in the context of taking oaths, a setting more than any other when honesty is expected to follow, Jesus says, "All you need to say is simply 'Yes' or 'No.'" (Mt. 5:37) In other words, Christians should be people of such integrity that we shouldn't even need to take oaths in the first place. Commenting on this passage, *The Interpreter's Bible* says, "God cannot be honored except by truth on the lips and truths in the heart."[76]

Christians should be known for their unswerving adherence to the truth and to honesty, *always*. No puffery or deception; no "staging" of your readiness that is in any way deceptive or misleading. Clayton Christensen said, "[I]t's easier to hold to your principles 100 percent of the time than it is to hold to them 98 percent of the time."[77] His point is that if you compromise yourself just once, it's more likely you will do so again.

And referring to Jesus' comment about "Yes" and "No," William Barclay says, "It leaves upon us the obligation to make ourselves such that

---

[76] *The Interpreter's Bible*, vol. 7, 300.
[77] Clayton Christensen: *How Will You Measure Your Life?* 191

men will so see our transparent goodness that they will never ask an oath of us..."[78]

This need for openness and transparency should be a permanent feature of all aspects of our lives, at all times. Our readiness as Christians should therefore be characterized by what ethicists call the sunshine principle: imagine that everything you did was known to everyone, with everything exposed to daylight and nothing hidden in darkness. Imagine your prospective boss saw you padding your resume. Or your prospective date saw you listing achievements on your online profile that you've distorted almost beyond recognition. The vital question is, "What if everyone knew the whole picture?"

There are also behaviors that scholars of interpersonal communication call "inappropriate self-disclosure." There's no need, for example, to mention in that job interview or on that online dating profile your occasional problems with constipation. There are limits to self-disclosure. But the question remains: "Is there anything in 'staging' yourself to be ready for this interaction that you hope the other person doesn't discover?" Everyone should be able to answer with confidence that there are neither pertinent omissions of the truth nor inclusions of deception. And for Christians, more than anyone, whatever staging we do should always be marked by "truth on the lips and truths in the heart."

---

[78] William Barclay: *Daily Study Bible: Matthew vol. 1*, 160.

37: A Reluctant Readiness

It is impossible to imagine a more harrowing command from God than this: "I want you to sacrifice your firstborn son, the one I have promised would be your heir and essential link in the chain that will make you a father of as many descendants as there are stars in the sky." Yet that is the horrific command God gives Abraham in Genesis 22. This command is all the more confounding because God seems to be undoing the miracle of enabling Abraham and Sarah to have a son in the first place, after years of infertility. "What on earth is God doing here?" Abraham must have thought, as God seemed to be destroying a plan so miraculously wrought.

But almost as astonishing as God's command is Abraham's unhesitating obedience. Note that his response is untainted by a desperate negotiation with God; instead, it is marked by a prompt and reluctant readiness to obey. He sets out with the boy and two servants the very next morning. Abraham packs what's needed and they set off. As they make their way to Mount Moriah, how he must have looked longingly at the son of his old age, the miracle baby now grown to boyhood, knowing this child is about to die. The journey is long; we're told that "on the third day..." (verse 4) Abraham sees the God-ordained site in the distance. The death of Isaac is imminent. Yet as Abraham's heart and head are silently screaming "No, Lord!" his faith and obedience prevail. The final leg of the journey is before them; there's no turning back now. And still Abraham's reluctant readiness to obey persists.

We know the rest of the story well. Just as Isaac's miraculous birth paralleled to some degree Jesus' miraculous conception, we see a parallel in death as well: Jesus escaped the stranglehold of death on the third day, just as Isaac's death sentence is revoked on the third day when Abraham discovers the ram caught by its horns.

Throughout the narrative we cannot avoid being stunned by Abraham's readiness to obey. God had singled out a man who initially obeys Him by leaving his home in Haran and going to an unknown land. As the writer to Hebrews puts it, "By faith Abraham, when called to go to a place he would later receive as his inheritance, obeyed and went, even though he did not know where he was going." (Heb. 11:8) Now, after several other stages on the journey in each of which he again readily obeyed the Lord, as outlined in Genesis 12, he settled in the Negev.

But these acts of obedience, costly though they were in pulling up stakes and heading into unknown territory and an unknown future, were small potatoes compared with this latest command. Chapter 22 begins, "Some time later God tested Abraham." Then comes the instruction to sacrifice Isaac. One finds among commentators on this passage that numerous issues swirl around this command. Did Abraham believe in advance that God was just testing him and that He would provide an animal to sacrifice? Or did he believe that even if he killed Isaac, that God would raise him from the dead? How was Abraham to relate this command to the common practice of child sacrifice among the Canaanites?

Regardless of these and other questions surrounding this episode, we inevitably return to Abraham's initial response of a ready, yet undoubtedly confused and reluctant, obedience. So deep was his faith, and so close his walk with the God Who had called him and led him this far, that he felt he had no choice but to honor this latest command.

Abraham's reluctant readiness was surpassed only by Jesus' commitment to an actual sacrifice: of Himself on the cross. In fact, we may do Abraham an injustice by describing him as "reluctant," which Merriam-Webster's online dictionary defines as "feeling or showing aversion, hesitation, or unwillingness."[79] Regardless of Abraham's feelings, it's astonishing that the Genesis account shows no sign of his "aversion, hesitation, or unwillingness." Clearly, this man of profound faith and who was so dependent on God knew what it meant to be ready – ready to sacrifice even his son because the God whom he trusted told him to do so.

~~~~~

Leon Uris (1923-2004) was an American writer best known for his novels.[80] In one of them, *Armageddon: A Novel of Berlin* (1963), he describes one aspect of how Nazi SS officers were trained to be ruthless. The recruits were each given a puppy to raise, supposedly to help them learn discipline. Then, after several months, each recruit was abruptly ordered to shoot the puppy. If they showed any reluctance, they were kicked out of the program. Their readiness to obey orders was paramount.

Whether this story has any basis in fact is disputed. Some versions say this occurred in the Hitler Youth program, which critics have said wasn't true. But regardless of how much Uris' description is based in fact (and apparently his historical novels were well researched), this tale holds an important lesson for Christians.

---

[79] https://www.merriam-webster.com/dictionary/reluctant. Accessed Oct. 6, 2023.
[80] This chapter is adapted from Gordon S. Jackson: *Your Photo on God's Fridge Door.*

God isn't in the business of asking us to shoot puppies. But as we reflect on what we hold most dear—our career, our family members, our health, our very lives—what are we willing to sacrifice if God called us to do so? So, how ready *are* we to obey God's unwelcome commands? Especially the really, really unwelcome ones?

May our faith be such that we could respond without "aversion, hesitation, or unwillingness."

38: Yes, And...

For God's son, Jesus Christ...was not one who vacillated between yes and no. It was always yes with him. He is the yes to all the promises of God.
                              — 2 Corinthians 1:20, William Barclay translation

The stage manager announces that it's "Five minutes to curtain." The show is about to begin. However, instead of a play in which everyone has prescribed lines and a clear part to play, this evening's performance promises a round of improv hilarity. Your improv troupe at the university is highly regarded so you are all the more grateful that you've been selected to participate tonight.

It's your debut with the group and as you reflect on what lies ahead, you go over in your mind the basics that were drilled into you in the troupe's rehearsals.

- Remember that this isn't an occasion for you to show how quick-witted you are; don't try to be funny or hog the limelight. Your job is to help all your partners shine.
- Remember the "*yes-and*" rule: Go with whatever line or situation a player hands you and respond so that whoever speaks next will be able to run with what you said.
- Don't ask questions unless you're also adding information; questions stifle the spontaneity and hamper the creativity.
- Establish for the audience a sense of relationship between all the players.
- Similarly, establish a sense of place.
- Finally, set up some kind of conflict or tension that will draw the audience in.

~~~~~

You remind yourself of these rules to calm your nerves. And you think again of the curious parallels between improv and your faith. You are reminded of the quote you encountered, by Ugo Betti, an Italian judge and playwright: "To believe in God is to know that all the rules will be fair and that there will be wonderful surprises." Not a bad description both of your faith and of good improv, you think. Your Christian life comes with no pre-ordained script; as with improv, you're going to make it up as you go, with one choice after another. Of course, the show tonight is pure entertainment, with what you hope will be wonderful surprises, for the performers and the audience. The choices you make to advance a humorous scene are of short-term consequence. Even so, given the need to make your partners look good, you see another parallel with your faith, this time with Paul's admonition to the Philippians to be humble: "In humility value others above yourselves, not looking to your own interests but each of you to the interests of the others." (Phil. 2:3-4)

Then, by definition, improv is a team sport; you don't do it alone. It requires a team of people who are committed to a common good: that of engaging in a particular type of live theater to amuse an audience. You think of tomorrow, when you'll attend church, and you're reminded of that verse in Hebrews where the writer emphasizes the need for Christians to keep getting together for worship. (Heb. 10:25) Just as you need your fellow performers tonight, even more do you need the support and encouragement of your fellow Christians.

Then you begin to wonder how a sense of place might apply to your faith and...

~~~~~

"One-minute to curtain!" comes the interruption. Time to end your musings. You head toward the stage. You know that the rehearsals, the practice drills in which your troupe engaged, and the trust you have established with each other have all prepared you for this moment. You're as ready as you can be for your improv debut tonight.

As you take your place on stage with the five other performers, it strikes you that you're even more ready than you thought for your real role in life: the one with eternal consequences, the role to which you've been called by God Himself. You don't know how that role will unfold, but you know it's being scripted by a God who promises you only good.

And as the MC announces the first game of the evening, you tell yourself once again: "Yes, and..."

PART 6: End Matters

39: The Second Coming, Prom Night, and Idols

No one prays for the second coming on prom night.

— *James Edwards*[81]

We like to think that idols are a thing of the past, or at least a thing of pagans in far off exotic countries. We therefore think that we could dispense with the commandment telling the Israelites to avoid idol worship in any form: "You shall have no other gods before me," says the second commandment. "You shall not make for yourself an image in the form of anything in heaven above or on the earth beneath or in the waters below." (Ex. 20:3-4)

If you define idols as those statues like the golden calf that got Aaron and the children of Israel in such trouble, then you're probably right. Most Western Christians don't have little statues in the homes, to whom they pray, offer gifts, or turn in times of trouble.

But a broader definition of "idol" would be anything that displaces God as the primary and exclusive focus of our allegiance. Yes, *anything*. That could include seemingly worthy or innocent things: sport, exercise, career, family, even ministry. Or it could be problematic things that have a grip on us, such as alcohol or visits to the casino.

Which leads us to this hypothetical: If you knew Jesus were going to return on prom night, would you be ready? One hundred percent ready? Or would you ask Him if He could please wait a day or two. (After all, you've looked forward to this event for so long and it would be such a shame to miss it.) Or how about your wedding? Or fiftieth wedding anniversary, with the Alaska cruise? Couldn't He wait till we get back? *Please....*

"Yes, I'm ready, Lord, but ..."

---

[81] James Edwards: sermon delivered in Spokane, WA; date unknown.

40: When the Hourglass Runs Out

Dag Hammarskjöld was a brilliant Swedish economist and diplomat, whose abilities led to his appointment at the young age of forty-seven as the Secretary General of the United Nations. Seen as a superb statesman and mediator, he was on his way to a peace mission in central Africa that involved UN troops, when his plane crashed in what is now Zambia. Controversy continues six decades later regarding the cause of the crash, with evidence that his Douglas DC-6 may have been shot down.[82]

After his death his diary was discovered and translated into English as *Markings*. One of his observations, ironic given the nature of his death in the service of peace, was: "The hardest thing of all—to die *rightly*.—An exam nobody is spared—and how many pass it? And you? You pray for strength to meet the test—but also for leniency on the part of the Examiner."[83]

That is the focus of this chapter: how to die *rightly* as a Christian. As Hammarskjöld says, death is the final exam that all of us face. The Christian, though, is able to prepare for this ultimate transition with a confidence and assurance that death is not the end. Christians of all traditions and denominations, whether Protestant, Catholic or Orthodox, share the profound belief that in death we enter eternal life, spared of further hurt or suffering and never to be separated from the presence of God Himself.

This assurance of eternal life comes directly from Jesus, on several occasions. For example, He promised His followers this future in heaven: "My Father's house has many rooms; if that were not so, would I have told you that I am going there to prepare a place for you?" (Jn. 14:2) Then there were Jesus' words on the cross to the penitent criminal crucified alongside Him: "Truly I tell you, today you will be with me in paradise." (Lk. 23:43)

While Christians can have full confidence in life after death, as Paul tells the Thessalonian believers (1 Thess. 4:13-18), what needs to be said about *preparing* to die? For we do it only once and, as Hammarskjöld indicates, we get only one chance at doing it *rightly*. That means at least doing the basics: ensuring that legal documents (a will, durable power of attorney, etc.) are complete and up to date; discussing with family

---

[82] For a discussion of this evidence see the Wikipedia entry on Hammarskjöld.
[83] Dag Hammarskjöld: *Markings*, 82.

members details about a funeral or memorial service; considering hospice care; ensuring that money matters are taken care of; and so on. Beyond these essential steps, there are other practical things that you could anticipate: ensuring that someone will return any outstanding library books or donating any air miles you have and won't be able to use. These steps assume that we will have time to make these preparations. Not all of us do. We therefore do well to heed the advice of Thomas à Kempis, who wrote: "Always be ready; always live in such a way that death can never find you unprepared."[84]

What if we layer on top of these steps a distinctively Christian dimension? What else would (or should) a Christian do as death approaches? The first step, which concerns our attitude and emotions, is to remind ourselves that, like Paul, Christians ought to see death as something to be welcomed: "For to me, to live is Christ and to die is gain." (Phil. 1:21) Naturally, we fear death, like all mortals. Yet Christ has secured our passage into a new world.

The English poet and cleric John Donne (1572-1631) put it like this in his brilliant sonnet, "Death be not proud":

One short sleep past, we wake eternally
And death shall be no more; Death, thou shalt die.[85]

And T. S. Eliot, also an English poet, offered another Christian perspective on death. In his play, *Murder in the Cathedral*, the Archbishop of Canterbury, Thomas Becket, is about to be assassinated. Aware of his fate, Becket says, "I am not in danger: only near to death."[86] That brief statement captures perfectly the Christian understanding of death. Given his impending assassination, Becket knows he is close to death but he is in no true danger because his soul is secure.

But if that is the mindset with which Christians can approach their own deaths, what practical things might they do that would also be distinctively Christian? One obvious step is confessing one's sins, either to a priest or a pastor, or privately to God. Another is to right any wrongs that are still lingering in your life. Are any letters of apology called for? Or how about thank-you letters or phone calls to people who shaped or enriched your life in ways they may not have realized? Yet other notes could go to close family members. Then, as the end approaches, you'll be saying goodbyes to those closest to you, assuming you are capable of doing so. Finally, you'll be heading home; you know the way.

---

[84] Thomas À Kempis, *The Imitation of Christ*. Translated by Betty Knott, 73.
[85] https://www.poetryfoundation.org/poems/44107/holy-sonnets-death-be-not-proud. Accessed April 18, 2024.
[86] T. S. Eliot: *Murder in the Cathedral*, 70.

Sometimes, though, death comes unexpectedly and without warning, with no time to prepare. Which brings us back to the advice of Thomas à Kempis: "Always be ready." Day by day, then, we can be utterly confident in the knowledge that nothing can separate us from His love. As Paul asked the Christians in Rome, "Who shall separate us from the love of Christ? ... I am convinced that neither death nor life ...will be able to separate us from the love of God that is in Christ Jesus our Lord." (Rom. 8:35-39) Having committed our lives to serving Christ, we are His, not to be snatched away under any circumstances. Not even death. Nor do we have to hope for "leniency on the part of the Examiner," as Hammarskjöld colorfully put it.[87] Jesus has in effect taken the exam on our behalf.

~~~~

A sign at a cemetery in Charleston, SC, notes the passing of a certain Colonel William Rhett: "He was born in London 4th Sept. 1666, Arrived and settled this Country 19th November 1694. And dyed suddenly but not unprepared 12 Janry 1722, In the fifty seventh year of his age."[88]

Note the wording: *"suddenly but not unprepared."* The length of our lives is measured in an hourglass; we see the bottom half reflecting the days, months and years we have lived. But the top half is hidden from us. We have no idea how much more sand will trickle through, marking the days that remain to us. Those last grains could come through tomorrow. Actuarial tables may tell us the odds are good we'll live another thirty, forty or fifty years. But those numbers are averages; we are unique individuals with unique lives, whose end isn't governed by statistics.

Whatever the means by which we will meet our end, whether it's sudden or following a long illness, Christians can be absolutely confident that our next step has been prepared for us. Just as God did for William Rhett.

---

[87] Dag Hammarskjöld: *Markings*, 82.
[88] The spelling, wording and punctuation are correct, reflecting the writing conventions of the early 1700s.

41: Conclusion: Onward Only With You

*Yahweh replied, "I myself will go with you, and I will give you rest." Moses
said, "If you are not going with us yourself, do not make us leave this place."*
— *Exodus 33:14-15*, Jerusalem Bible

In this passage we have Moses telling God (1) that he has heard and
understood the promise that God will accompany the Israelites until their
journey's end, and (2) that there's no point going any further without
God's divine presence. We know that Moses' motivation for saying what
he does in Part 2 is not mere politeness, along the lines of, "Oh, come on,
it won't be the same without You." No, Moses knows that without God's
leadership and presence, the Israelites' journey is pointless. God alone can
bring them safely to the Promised Land; He is the one who has called them
out of Egypt and led them safely thus far, with one desert miracle after
another beginning with the crossing of the Red Sea. Even if they were
confident of making it past the hazards that undoubtedly lay ahead
without God's help, Yahweh was their *God*; how could they possibly part
ways and leave Him behind? Under these conditions, then, Moses says
that he and the Israelites are ready to move on.

With us too, how can we even imagine continuing our life's journey
by parting company with God? "Thanks, Lord, for everything so far. But
we're going to strike out on our own now." For anyone to think of turning
one's back on God in that way is breathtaking. For those of us who, like
the Israelites, have been rescued and redeemed from our equivalent of
Egypt, to shrug off our God is beyond belief. How can we turn our back
on the God of whom hymn-writer Robert Grant said:

Your mercies, how tender, how firm to the end,
Our Maker, Defender, Redeemer, and Friend!

Moses affirms that there's no point going forward without the
presence of Yahweh, knowing that God's mercies will be with them until
the end of their journey. Nor will those mercies cease when the Israelites
reach Canaan. We too are ready to move on but without You guiding us,
what would be the point? Without You, how *could* we be truly ready?

We have the assurance that God will lead and accompany us; we've
walked with God long enough to know there'd be no point continuing our
faith journey on our own and leaving behind our maker, defender,
redeemer and friend.

Acknowledgements

As with each of my books, others have played a significant role in shaping the manuscript, identifying errors that had repeatedly escaped me, and offering suggestions for improvement. Among those who were most helpful were Mildred Basing, K. G. Kim, Jeremy Fortleigh-Brigham, Hans Pieter Schragg, and Beddo Vermeulen. I am much in their debt.

My son, Matthew Jackson, once again brought his uncanny proofreading skills to bear on the manuscript's imperfections. Any errors that remain are my responsibility alone, of course, although I'm still hoping to place the blame elsewhere.

About the Author

Gordon S. Jackson is an author and educator who was born and grew up in South Africa. After receiving his undergraduate education in Cape Town, he obtained his MA from Wheaton College, IL, and his doctorate in mass communication at Indiana University. He taught journalism at Whitworth College in Spokane, WA for thirty-two years until his retirement. He is married to another South African, who helps keep his accent honest. They have two adult children and identical twin granddaughters.

Always Ready is his twenty-second book and his fourth with Mt. Zion Ridge Press.

THANK YOU!

Thank you for reading this book from Mt. Zion Ridge Press.

If you enjoyed the experience, learned something, gained a new perspective, or made new friends through story, could you do us a favor and write a review on Goodreads or wherever you bought the book?

Thanks! We and our authors appreciate it.

We invite you to visit our website, MtZionRidgePress.com, and explore other titles in fiction and non-fiction. We always have something coming up that's new and off the beaten path.

And please check out our podcast, Books on the Ridge, where we chat with our authors and give them a chance to share what was in their hearts while they wrote their book, as well as fun anecdotes and glimpses into their lives and experiences and the writing process. And we always discuss a very important topic: *Tea!*

You can listen to the podcast on our website or find it at most of the usual places where podcasts are available online. Please subscribe so you don't miss a single episode!

Thanks for reading. We hope you come back soon!

www.ingramcontent.com/pod-product-compliance
Lightning Source LLC
Chambersburg PA
CBHW010939120626
46554CB00008B/2539